A New Way to Ride

Listening and Following

Judy Ceppa

RonJon Publishing, Inc.

Photographs by Judith Rountree Ceppa

Scripture taken from the *Holy Bible, New International Version*. Copyright c 1973, 1978, 1984 International Bible Society. Used by permission of Zondervan Bible Publishers.

© 2005 Judith Rountree Ceppa

ISBN 1-56870-561-1

First Edition

Printed in the United States of America

RonJon Publishing, Inc.
1001 S. Mayhill Rd.
Denton, Texas 76208
(940) 383-3060
Information@ronjonpublishing.com

All rights reserved. This book or parts thereof may not be reproduced or used in any form or by any means—graphic, electronic or mechanical, including photocopying, recording, taping or information storage and retrieval systems—without written permission of the publisher. Making copies of this book, or any portion, is a violation of United States copyright laws.

"The poetic meditations of Judy Ceppa are truly a God-inspired travelogue. Her journey with her husband Fred across America reveals to the reader not only the beauty of our great land, but a deeply-felt spiritual link with God's creation. This is a book to treasure. Her words have captured the soul of nature and God's gift to all Americans."

G. William Whitehurst, United States Congressman (Ret.)

"The unfolding metaphor of Judy and Fred Ceppa's tour on their Gold Wing grows out of the acute awareness of the natural world possible on a bike ride. As they explore "a new way to ride," "listening and following," their journey becomes a metaphor for a spiritual journey. Judy hears a message in every scene, every turn of weather, every surprise of the road. As she discovers ecstasy in the beauty of nature, she finds herself learning to listen more closely. She becomes more attentive to each moment, and learns the need to let go of control. She discovers that this new way to ride "has taken hold of us as a new way of living." I am inspired by Judy's delight in nature and her ability to read wisdom in it for the journey of life."

Frances Irene Taber, Ohio Yearly Meeting (Conservative)

"Even though her sparkling prose and rich poetry transform scene and sound into a verbal landscape, at its heart, Judith's book is the diary of a spiritual journey by two seasoned Quakers who respond to a divine call. *A New Way to Ride: Listening & Following* is an unlikely but refreshing look at ways to practice the Presence of God wherever we are. Readers will "ride the ride" vicariously with the author but, more importantly, will be invited to listen and follow as they travel on their own life journeys."

Tom Mullen, Author of A VERY GOOD MARRIAGE

To Fred

*~ my husband, companion, and friend ~
who with gentle alertness
drove our motorcycle on this journey
as we shared deep awareness of
God's presence in the creation
and the joy of this new way to ride:
listening and following.*

Table of Contents

In Gratitude... vii

Foreword... xi

Introduction... xvii

Chapter 1
  The Dream 1

Chapter 2
  Poetry, Beauty, Family 9

Chapter 3
  Creation Speaks 21

Chapter 4
  Desert Blessing 31

Chapter 5
  Interlude 43

Chapter 6
  Death Valley & Life 53

Chapter 7
  Blessed Interruption 67

Chapter 8
    Creation's Healing Love 81

Chapter 9
    Covenant 95

Chapter 10
    Turning Point 113

Chapter 11
    Spirit's Roadmap Brings Joy 127

Chapter 12
    The Shapes of God 145

Chapter 13
    The Journey Continues 161

Notes 177

Appendix A 179

Map 185

In Gratitude

The process by which this book came into being has been, in itself, a journey of *listening and following*. I offer heart-felt gratitude to the many people, whose encouragement and help along the path, have given me the courage to stay the course until this project reached fruition. I wish that I could name them all, but doing that would require a book in itself.

Long before the idea of a book was conceived, the prayers of close spiritual friends, my Spiritual Formation group, and our Silent Retreat community supported us throughout our journey. Being faithful to my commitment to share the messages I received as we traveled, I began to regularly e-mail home some of my reflections. I was humbled by the enthusiasm with which they were received. Soon the question began to arise: "Are you going to compile these into a book?" I offer thanks to those friends and family who were led to plant this seed and to nurture it when we returned home.

First among these is my friend, and former colleague, Barbara Aspinall. I am deeply grateful for her willingness to drag her "red pen" out of retirement and tackle the job of editing the original manuscript. With grace and humor, Barbara used her considerable expertise to guide me through multiple revisions as I struggled to turn my journal scribbling into proper prose and poetic form. Any lingering errors must be attributed to my failure to learn my lessons well, not to my patient teacher. Her enthusiasm for the completed manuscript and her recommendation that I seek publication opened a vista I had not at all envisioned for this simple journal. I am very grateful that she continued to work with me as the project progressed.

I owe a deep well of gratitude to all of those who were led to companion us spiritually, and in concrete physical ways, as I waded through the morass of the seeking-publication process.

My special thanks to those who, without hesitation, agreed to read the manuscript. I am particularly appreciative of the helpful comments of Judith Anderson, Ellen Cronin, Phil Johnson, and Ron Mattson.

To several people, I owe an even greater debt of gratitude. Without their encouragement in the early stages of this project and their faithful support and confidence throughout this long process, the will of this unproven author would surely have failed.

.... Tom Mullen of The Earlham School of Religion, who expressed such faith in the message and potential for this book, gave so very generously of his time and professional skills to do the final edit of the manuscript, offered unfailing interest and encouragement, and then graciously offered an endorsement for the book.

.... Nick Hoppner, editor of *Wing World Magazine*, whose unvarnished enthusiastic response to the manuscript offered a great moment of joy when he said, "this book must not be hidden under a basket," who independently sought out possibilities for publication, gave persistent prompting to "get on" with the project, and without a moment's hesitation took time from his already overcrowded schedule to lend his name to the project by writing the Foreword for the book.

.... Fran Taber of Ohio Yearly Meeting (Conservative), who carved out time from her busy schedule and drew upon her many talents to help and encourage the ministry of the author by critiquing the manuscript and then offering an endorsement for the book.

.... Dr. G. William Whitehurst of Old Dominion University, whose initial deeply moving spiritual response to the manuscript humbled me greatly, who provided an honest professional evaluation of the publishing potential, and affirmed that evaluation by writing an endorsement for the book. Dr. Bill and his wife Janie expressed an unfailing faith in the book's potential and have offered an undergirding foundation of confidence and spiritual support.

I owe my deepest gratitude to my husband, Fred, for his patience, his strong support, his never wavering faith in the message of our book, and his firm belief that we are being led to seek publication.

I would like to offer thanks to Gary and Patti Stratford for leading us to RonJon Publishing, Inc. A special thanks is owed Chrystal Tsiatsos for her friendly and professional help with our book throughout the publishing process with RonJon.

Finally, I offer humble gratitude to God, Who called us forth on this journey, Who graced my writing with the gift of poetry, Who remained faithful to speak the Word to us through the glories of creation, and Who used this journey to lead us into a new way to live. We have tried to *listen and follow* the divine "nudges" leading us to believe that we are not to keep this book "hidden under a basket."

Judy Ceppa
Second Month, 2005

Foreword

As editor of *Wing World*, the monthly magazine of the Gold Wing Road Riders Association, I've read thousands of accounts of people's travels aboard the ultimate touring motorcycle produced by Honda. Invariably, they focus on the roads ridden, weather endured, and the adventures they encounter along the way. Most of these memoirs are eminently forgettable, and very few come close to being philosophical or literary achievements.

The most notable exception to this prosaic trend, of course, is *Zen and the Art of Motorcycle Maintenance* by Robert Persig, a much-studied dissertation on Aristotelian versus Platonic philosophies barely supported by the writer's father-and-son search for cross-generational understanding while on a cross-country motorcycle trip. Persig's odyssey may not be easy reading, but neither is it easily forgotten by those thoughtful and intelligent enough to take the time to ponder its depths. Like a gravel gouge in your bike's paint, Persig's book stays with you for as long as you ride, forever changing your motorcycling experience.

Likewise, Judith Ceppa's *A New Way To Ride: Listening and Following* is just such a book. It will change your life, too, if you let it, yet in a far different way.

Judy Ceppa and her husband Fred are devout followers of the Holy Spirit. As members of the Religious Society of Friends (Quakers) they believe an element of God's spirit is implanted within every person's soul. They believe that while each of us has the innate inner capacity to comprehend what God's spirit would have us do, most of us are too busy following the dictates of our own agendas and thoughts to hear or follow the divine whispers within us. In what most of us would deem a gutsy move, Judy and Fred embraced the leadership of their God, and they embarked on a remarkable cross-country tour on their Gold Wing with the route and destinations, the pace and the detours determined by the still small voice within.

As if in divine response to this act of faith, Judy suddenly and mysteriously was enabled to write poetry. Scribbling in a small notebook while Fred piloted their 900-pound motorcycle, Judy recorded her thoughts over a four month, eleven thousand mile journey. Her verses tumble out in a variety of forms—free verse, rhymed stanzas, couplets. Much of her poetry is specific to the events of her trip, yet much is also universal. Like the Bible's *Book of Psalms*, all of Judy's verses speak directly to her and our often-veiled attempts to communicate back and forth with our Maker.

Here in the early years of the 21st Century, few readers make time to settle down by the fireside with a book of poetry. Yet the appeal of poetry prevails. Rhymed words abound in songs and advertising jingles in radio and television. A whole generation of young people has made the heavy cadences and rhymes of rap their personal soundtrack for life. And whenever we are moved by a tragedy, we seek a special way to convey our thoughts; not surprisingly, poetry is often the medium. So poetry is not something foreign—it is all around us. Alas, much bad poetry exists. What distinguishes the poetry of Judy Ceppa is its grace, its high quality, its natural voice and seemingly effortless word choice. The lady knows her craft.

Is *A New Way To Ride: Listening and Following* just a book for motorcyclists? Or is it a book just for poetry lovers? Or is it a book just for religious seekers and spiritual seekers?

The answer is, of course, that it is a book for *all* of these audiences—and hopefully more.

I invite you to read this book a little at a time. Set it aside and then come back to it. Read it in the quiet of the morning or the stillness of the night. If you have visited some of the places mentioned in this book, let Judy's words recall your own experiences. If she writes of places you've never seen, let her words paint portraits of grandeur in your mind. Most of all, as you read of her own very human struggles to follow the dictates of the spirit within, recognize and confront your own approach to the Divine Mystery.

I hope you find this book the graceful and thoughtful treasure I have. May you read and ride in wisdom and health.

Nick Hoppner
Editor, *Wing World*

*"Whether you turn to the right or to the left,
your ears will hear a Voice behind you saying,
'This is the way; walk in it."*

Isaiah 30:21

INTRODUCTION

Late in the morning of June 25, we guided our Honda Gold Wing motorcycle into the driveway of our Northern Virginia home. It had been exactly four months since we rode out to begin our 11,367 mile journey around the perimeter of the United States ~ quite an adventure for this aging couple! The wonder of it all was that instead of landing on our doorstep exhausted we returned home refreshed, filled with awe, spiritually renewed, and anxious to go again.

Our gentle homecoming was a direct consequence of the "new way to ride" we had only recently discovered and embraced. This discovery was a graced Gift that opened the way to fulfill our long held dream of a motorcycle tour around the nation at the very moment this dream coalesced with our *call* to become *traveling contemplatives*. This new way of touring required that we give up control of the ride and accept being *led* into the path we were to follow. Though we had a general sense of where we wanted to go and a tentative time frame, we rejected the inflexible scheduling of our traditional touring pattern and allowed our divine Guide to chart our course each day. It quickly became obvious to us that living into this "new way" would be a learning process, requiring patient waiting and listening for guidance. These attributes became the staples of our practice throughout our trip. We were often bewildered and confused by the abrupt changes in plans or direction into which we were guided. Eventually designated as "God's detours," these changes tested our willingness to trust Divine guidance. Sometimes it seemed we were stumbling in the dark. Then a clear sense would arise that "this is the way; walk in it."

As our hearts and heads remained quiet enough to hear the divine Voice speaking through the world of nature, we became more aware of our spiritual unity with all of creation. Each of the places to which we were led offered unique blessings for our individual spiritual journeys. Death Valley and Shelter Cove provided special experiences of growth and awareness of Divine love. The Redwoods offered sanctuaries of solitude and graced places of peace. The desert afforded the stillness and silence just to *be* in the Creator's healing presence. The mountains lifted our spirits in joy. The coast baptized us in its beauteous waves. The high plains stretched our souls to eternity. The lakes settled us in tranquil calm. The great Niagara River immersed our spirits in wonder and the joy of surrendering control of our lives to God.

The entire trip was an epiphany opening our spirits to a new awareness of the Sacred in all of life and of our connection with the created world. Little did we realize these four months would result in changing the way we live our lives. Such, however, has been the case. This transformation is the flowering of seeds planted along the way as we were touched by wonder, embraced by the Holy in the scenes before us, and as we listened to Spirit's whisperings in the wind. Though we journeyed on a motorcycle, this approach to touring can guide any travel plans whatever the means of transportation and waiting for retirement years is not a necessity; age is not a factor. Nor must one be traveling to enter this new way to ride because it is in truth a way of living, of "practicing the presence of God" as Brother Lawrence said.* Children, adults, and aging grandparents will enjoy learning to be present to the Creator through the wonders of nature whether a majestic Redwood tree is sheltering them or the little saplings sprouting from a decaying log entrance them. All can learn to be still and listen to the Spirit's guidance for the path we are to travel, the steps we are to take. The only condition governing the reception of these gifts is the willingness to slow down and open one's eyes, ears, and heart to what is given. God chooses many different ways of bringing persons into intimate relationship with the Divine.

We share in this book the joy of our experience. We hope our journey will speak to your spirit and be an invitation to adventure into the joy of this *new way to ride ~ listening and following*. We pray God's blessings upon *your* journey.

Judith Ceppa

The Dream & The Call

A sense of wonder surrounds my reflection as I review the path by which God brought us to this journey. This reminiscence offers a glimpse of how patiently the Spirit works to fulfill the Divine purpose for our lives. From deep within memory rises an event that, in retrospect, was the first intimation urging us to "the way" of listening and following.

While planning for a tour of Colorado, my husband, Fred, and I searched for stories of interesting motorcycle rides. An article highlighting the gravel road leading down the face of Grand Mesa caught Fred's attention. This article's description of the road as "not for the faint-hearted," filled me with a foreboding sense of misadventure. Fred's reaction was quite different. He was very excited about riding that road. Because he is a careful motorcyclist not given to taking risks, I dismissed my discomfort as nervousness about the unknown.

When our tour of Colorado became a reality, the fateful day arrived for our ride across Grand Mesa and down the winding road on its face. That morning the fearful brooding overtook my spirit once again. Heightening the sense of danger, rains came during the night and continued to fall. Locked into a short vacation schedule, we lacked the flexibility to say, "Let's just wait a day." Since the rain was only a light drizzle, we donned our rain suits, mounted the bike, and headed out.

At the top of Grande Mesa, we found a hard-packed, maroon/gray dirt and gravel road. The misty rain clinging to the windshield and our helmet face shields blended into the gravel scene and made visibility very difficult. Trusting in Fred's driving skills, I smothered my fears and my feeling that we should not be riding this road. When a car approached from the opposite direction, we flagged the driver down. Fred asked if the road down the face of the Mesa would be safe for us. She assured us the road was fine and we would have no problem. Cautiously, we continued on.

Suddenly the motorcycle sank into a huge pothole filled with fresh, loose gravel. The bike had no traction in this milieu; controlling the steering was virtually impossible. Before Fred could hit the kill switch and halt the bike, the front wheel hit solid ground under the gravel. The wheel gripped the hard dirt and with a mighty thrust forward threw the bike, the trailer, and us across the road. Fortunately we landed on grass and neither of us was hurt. The bike was terribly scratched, but not seriously damaged. The trailer was torn from the hitch. The question now was how to lift this nearly half-ton motorcycle to an upright position.

Mercifully, in our moment of need, guardian angels appeared in an old pick-up truck. The couple stopped, helped us right the bike and reattach the trailer. We asked about riding the road down the front of the Mesa. The expression on the husband's face told me my sense of dread was not unfounded. Obviously astounded, he responded: "You do not want to ride that road with this rig! I've seen riders with much smaller bikes than yours drop their motorcycles on that road. Why don't you follow us to the Lodge, have lunch, rent a cabin here, and just enjoy the beauty of the Mesa." We accepted the couple's gracious invitation, enjoyed the hour's conversation with them during lunch, but decided to rent a room in town for the night. Waving good-bye to our benefactors, we agreed to return their favor by helping someone else who might be in need.

Riding down from Grande Mesa on the main road, we soon arrived in the valley. Stopping at the visitor's center to inquire about motels, we saw a large map depicting the road we had planned to ride as an intricate weaving of hairpin turns and switchbacks. On that gravel road, in a misty rain, our ride would truly have been a frightening, dangerous, and possibly fatal journey. When we checked into the motel that evening, Fred, who is extremely solicitous of his machines, looked at our poor scratched and scarred Gold Wing and despairingly announced: "I'm not even going to cover it." I reminded him the fall and resulting damage were not the bike's fault. The tenderness that is so much a part of Fred then surfaced; he smiled and said, "You're right." We carefully covered our Wing for its night's rest. Before retiring, we made a promise not to ride on dirt and gravel roads again. We were very thankful to be safe.

As we now review our determined desire to ride that road, we recognize our refusal to acknowledge the Spirit's invitation to *listen*. Feelings of discomfort were ignored. A dangerous rain situation was underestimated. We now believe these forebodings were gentle Divine "nudges" seeking to keep us on a safe path. Finally it seemed the Divine exasperation shouted: "If I throw you off the bike will you pay attention to My warnings?" Although at the time we would not have articulated our experience in these terms, we now know we were being told to become more attentive to Spirit's whisperings in our motorcycle touring and in our lives.

God's "nudges" continued to press upon our spirits ~ unsought, at first unrecognized, and then unacknowledged for what they were. Over a period of nine years, however, we became more receptive in listening to these Divine "nudges." A growing awareness of Spirit's active presence radically changed the inner landscape of our lives. As a result, our lifestyle also changed.

Finding a new touring pattern became an essential part of our new, simpler, more reflective life. Through the years our motorcycle touring was enjoyable, but because of jobs, family obligations, and our accustomed touring pattern, we often returned home exhausted, hardly ready for a return to our harried work schedules. When we retired, our trips became more pleasant as we were no longer pushed by deadlines. We still found it difficult, however, to discard our learned pattern of riding that called for a definite length of time to be away, a trip plan of places to visit and stay, and a specific number of miles to be covered each day. There was little flexibility or time for reflection and stillness to simply be in God's presence and listen.

Our inability to let go of this structured touring pattern was negatively impacting our dream of a motorcycle ride around the perimeter of the United States with side trips to sites calling to us. We wondered whether such a trip were even possible for us because we were aging and beset by ailments often accompanying that stage of life. Our tightly scheduled touring style was not conducive to accommodating these life changes in the lengthy journey we envisioned. We finally decided we simply could not manage an adventure of this magnitude. The dream, however, would not die. Consequently, we decided to take an extended autumn motorcycle tour of the Finger Lakes and Adirondack areas of New York. Ostensibly this trip was undertaken to enjoy the beauty of the countryside. In truth, we hoped to discover a touring style relaxing enough to let us venture forth on our dream-ride. To assure the best opportunity for a leisurely experience, we informed family and friends that we did not know when we would return but would remain in contact through e-mail. Rejecting our usual touring pattern, we simply went where we felt *led* to go and stayed over if we began to tire. We were given far more than we had hoped for in this trip.

As we traveled, we became amazed at the beautiful and meaningful places to which we were led. In the splendor of this land, we felt the Creator's presence as being very close. The Spirit seemed to guide us and speak through the natural world. I recorded these powerful messages faithfully in my journal. Once again, I began to sense Divine "nudges." I wrote: "God has been imprinting a quiet message upon my life as we have traveled this month. I am being called to become a *traveling contemplative* ~ to travel, to drink in the spiritual messages emanating from the created world, to write of the impact of these messages upon my life, and to share these" (*Journal*, September 6, 2000). When we returned home rested, renewed, and our lives so spiritually enriched, we knew we had been given "a new way to ride."

Feeling led to take another look at our dreamed-of trip around the nation, we sought guidance through prayer and eventually felt we were meant to undertake this journey. As though to authenticate this conviction, other people suddenly offered to assume several of our major commitments while other obligations simply expired. As Quakers say, "way opened." With great enthusiasm, we began to make preparations for our ride.

During the months readying for our tour, my "call" to become a *traveling contemplative* was reaffirmed. This had emerged as a strange call for me, one I could not have anticipated. Several years earlier when we traveled to visit California's Redwoods and Ancient Bristlecone Pines, I had felt a similar call for that specific time. Now the call was clearer and more generalized, a call to a *way of being*.

> "We have different gifts according to the grace given us....
> Use [your gift] in proportion to your faith."
>
> *- Romans 12:6*

> I heard God's voice, it was so clear:
> "Listen child! Try to really hear.
>   I have a task for you to do,
>   one to which I've called very few.
> You are to travel throughout this land
>   and listen for My message in all that I planned.
> Creation will speak the words you are to write
>   to tell of the beauty, variety, and sights
>   of the abundance I offer to meet all need,
>   if only humankind is willing to heed
>   My way of love and community.

"Some will say you're not doing a thing,
    but only on vacation and having a fling.
Don't mind those harsh words.
    Stay the course I have given
    for with many different gifts
    humankind I have leavened.
I have called *you* to contemplation;
    just trust, follow, and do not question.

What I do with this call is Mine to decide!
Your task is only in My presence to abide."

We took to the road in response to this call,
And trusted God's lead to take care of it all.

With a powerful commitment to live into this "new way to ride" and with a deep sense of purpose and of being *led*, we arrived at the day set for departure on our journey.

Poetry, Beauty, Family

Following a fitful night's sleep, we wake on February 25th filled with anticipation and anxious to begin our journey. We open the curtains and our spirits momentarily fail.

> The day is cold,
> > damp,
> > gray.
> Spirits are swayed
> > by clouds of doubt.

Throughout the morning a chill, heavy winter rain falls. Such a downpour does not invite climbing on the motorcycle and beginning our journey. Our bags are packed, we are ready to go, but our departure is foiled by a winter storm. Will we get away at all? What message are we being given?

Before we even begin our journey, we are called upon to practice the discipline of letting go of what we want and plan. We faced this same necessity as we packed. We have only two saddlebags, a trunk, and a small motorcycle trailer for the six-month journey we envision. The process of choosing what physical possessions to take is a spiritual challenge, that of deciding what is really important to us. We are honestly surprised to find how little is necessary. Devotional books, our Bibles, and my journal are priority. Laptop computers are needed for my writing and our e-mail contacts. A 35mm camera will preserve the visual memories that may fade with time. Clothes choices are simplified by our "plain dress," but are complicated by the necessity to accommodate riding temperatures varying from chill winter cold to desert summer heat. Rounding out the list are supplies for our 4 a.m. morning coffee and food for simple breakfasts and suppers. Since our bags are already packed, we proceed, in spite of the rain, to load the bike and trailer.

Committed to *listening and following,* we do not succumb to disappointment. We will see what the rest of the day brings. As we wait, delicious turkey sandwiches perk up our metabolism and our spirits. By early afternoon, the rain abates. Excitedly, we ready ourselves to ride. The temperature is only forty-four degrees and the wind chill factor on a moving motorcycle calls for warm clothing under our rain suits. After a final check on the house, a quick kiss, and a moment of silent prayer, we pull on our full-face helmets and connect our intercom. I climb on the Gold Wing behind Fred and we exit our driveway.

> Mist and chill
> greet our ride;
> hearts trust
> this is God's will.

We ride only sixty miles before the rain returns just after we pull off the road for a cup of coffee. The motel across the parking lot from where we are stopped is a welcome sight. A soft sofa, a luxurious king-size bed, and a steaming cup of coffee provide the setting for a relaxing evening. Our long dreamed-of ride has begun.

> Falling rain bathes us
> in misty blessing.
>> Coffee break,
>> a quiet room,
>> gentle rest,
>> spirits free.
>> All is well.

Poetry, Beauty, Family

Recording this first day's events and impressions in my journal, I am surprised as poetry flows from my pen. I had looked forward to this time away for contemplation, peace, and writing, not considering the form this writing would take. This gift of verse is totally unexpected and seems a graced affirmation of our *leading* to make this journey. Filling several journal pages allows my exhilaration to calm. Finally, the adrenaline stops pumping and we turn in for the night.

When we wake to the new day,

> morning breaks glorious,
> sunshine and warmth.
> Spirits respond
> to God's call to go forth.

We are impatient to have breakfast and be on the road. We offer a grateful prayer for the loveliness of this day. The noise and busyness of the interstate highway fail to dampen our joy. Our hearts thrill with expectation! As we ride, our spirits mirror the changing landscape:

> Oh, joy of spring
> in blossoms white, across the dreary land
> of winter's night,
> speaks songs of rapture
> and of peace
> as hearts rise gently to Spirit's release.

> The path unclear ~
> mystery abounds.
> Your voice is clear in silence sounds.
> We need but follow
> the steps laid out and glorious surprises
> make spirits shout
> with joy and wonder and songs of praise.

A New Way to Ride–Listening and Following

> And though we ride into Mystery's mist,
> The ship of our lives will never list.
> Patient trust will carry all
> If only we center upon God's call.
>
> After three days of steady riding,
> winter's barrenness
> ~ cold, ice, snow ~
> recedes into memory's mist.
> Now moments fill
> with warm clime's glow.

Columbia, South Carolina, greets us with a springtime world. We have promised ourselves not ride every day on this tour; when it feels "right," we will take a time-out day. To remain true to our commitment to *listen and follow,* we need time for quiet reflection, to rest our bodies, and assimilate the experiences we are having. Since Lenten season is beginning, it seems an appropriate time to take the first break and share with one another our thoughts, hopes, and expectations. In this springtime world of South Carolina, the changing weather and landscape carry a vision of what this journey may hold for us.

> Across the land blossoms of pear and cherry
> stand in virgin white against bare trees
> while forsythia's gold
> melts winter's freeze.
>
> Peach trees cup pruned branches
> toward heaven in prayer,
> ask with blossoms their bareness to leaven.
> Pink buds appear,
> the blush of God's answering glow,
> the beauty of Divine creation shows.
>
> Pink/purple flowers of tulip trees
> bend and sway

Poetry, Beauty, Family

with each new breeze.
Pansies with their tiny faces
like divine rainbows
shower with grace.

Daffodils sway
shiny bright heads of yellow and white
in field and garden beds.
And deep rose/purple of beauty-berry!
A riot of color
Creator's world to make merry.

God's infinite love for diversity appears
As winter weeps joyous retreating tears.

Journal, February 25th-28th

Our contemplative sojourn in Columbia ends after our quiet morning meditation time. The sun glistens as we travel the interstate highway to Madison, Georgia, and happily anticipate the visit with my son's family. We especially look forward to being with our lively grandsons who love the idea that Gramma and Grampa tour the country on a motorcycle. The boys have a collection of smaller bikes, but we cannot interest them in a ride on the Gold Wing.

The initial happy greetings of arrival over, we spend the early evening visiting in their yard. Cutting through the laughter and fun, the sound of a distant train whistle summons the shadow lying over this visit; my children's father is in the last stages of terminal cancer.

Dusk train's mournful wail
Tears from deep within again
Death's train calls to all.

During our last night in Madison, the children receive the sad news of their father's death. In the morning my son and his family prepare to travel north. We will leave to ride south. Before we take to the road, however, we share together a joyful celebration for our grandsons' birthdays. This juxtaposition of birth and death is a powerful reminder. God is present with us in both happiness and sadness.

We ride quiet back roads leading to Valdosta, Georgia. My mind is filled with sad reflection. Perhaps the timing of this visit has more Divine guidance in it than I was aware. My family has experienced the painful consequences of divorce: alienation and broken relationships that have never yielded to Love's healing balm. Communication between family members has suffered greatly, especially during the last few months. The death of my children's father brings to the surface again and exacerbates all the ache of this brokenness. God has much healing to do in my heart to bring me to a place of peace and love.

Where this restorative work must begin is revealed in today's Scripture reading, which speaks of Moses' humility: "Moses was a very humble man, more humble than anyone on the face of the earth" (Numbers 12:3). A quiet prayer rises from my heart:

> Humility is the condition I seek,
> for ego wants to guide my path.
> Be small; trust that God will send
> His Spirit to rest upon the meek.
>
> This time apart, time to gain perspective,
> to gentle my heart and teach me patience;
> to learn to love without expectation,
> my actions filtered through God's pure sieve.
>
> Oh Father, take from my heart unkind judgment.
> Help me know this inner pain is Your aid
> to help me see Your guidance more clearly;
> renew my spirit and bring fresh commitment.

Poetry, Beauty, Family

> Your ways are couched in mystery.
> I seek to understand,
> but am given to be still and follow the cloud
> until chosen in secret Your way to see.
>
> Let my heart reside in Your house of joy,
> morning praises sing, evening songs of gratitude.
> May I dwell on Your mountain close to Your Spirit,
> Your indwelling presence write my spiritual story.

The evening is filled with reflection, reading, and prayer. Morning finds me more at peace. I must trust God to work in all this pain and bring healing. Leaving Valdosta, our ride flows gently through rural southern Georgia. The landscape itself reaches out to ease my sadness.

> Wisteria drips
> soft lavender tears,
> touching the spring earth
> with beauty.
> Pastel petals cover
> dark fears,
> gracing the earth
> with serenity.
> God's promised joy
> revealed through the years.
>
> Dogwood blossoms
> so brilliantly pure,
> bringing sparkle
> to earth's awakening.
> Their light shines forth
> earth's winter to lure,
> unfolding new life
> and blessing.
> God's promised love
> heart's pain will cure.

The sun warms my spirit and dries my tears. Our journey continues to the home of Fred's brother and his wife in McAlpin, Florida. The quiet rural setting of their home calms my aching heart. This peaceful place offers haven from city noise and lights. In the early morning dark, we sit under the cloudless star-filled sky. God's presence is very real.

Even this early morning time fails, however, to squelch my eventual longing to "get moving." I am finding it very difficult to remain faithful to living into our "new way." The pleasure of conversation, side trips into the community, wonderful meals, and puzzle solving begins to pale. Long walks under the towering trees are calming, but I am impatient and anxious to continue our journey. Major storms, however, are blowing in from the West. I am challenged to accept that, for whatever reason, we are not yet supposed to move on. Our original agreement was not to be rushed on this trip, but to travel as we are *led*. I go out on the deck that surrounds our family's home and immerse myself in the beauty of their acreage and the blessing of

> The long awaited rain that comes,
>   cooling the earth
>   from morning sun.
> Hushed stillness welcomes the dropping rain,
>   blue sky has faded,
>   clouds have gained.
> Whispered winds rustle towering trees
>   in fluttering dance
>   gifting earth with leaves.
> Gray-bearded moss graces ancient boughs.
>   Palmetto leaves
>   stand tall and proud.
> Birds huddle on branches and quiet their song,
>   red cardinal bows head,
>   for shelter he longs.
> Dampness enhances the sweet smell of earth.
>   From ground, drinking raindrops,

> this aroma is birthed.
> Rain is manna from heaven to this drought-stricken land,
> > a cool dripping grace
> > released from God's hand.

This grace becomes a cooling balm for my anxiety. I am being taught two important lessons. One is *patience*. Our divine Guide will not adhere to my desired time schedule. I must learn to let go and listen for the Spirit's timing and inspiration to tell us when to travel. The second lesson is *awareness*, an important discipline if I am to be faithful to my *call* to be a *traveling contemplative*. I must be able to set aside all kinds of distractions that fill my mind and be present to the moment. A different kind of awareness is also needed if we are to be safe on this journey. Awareness of the road, ~ ahead of us, around us, and behind us ~ is extremely important. Riding lonely by-ways is a luxury because Fred does not have to be as intently aware of traffic and can be more present to the beauty of our surroundings.

While these lessons take shape in my heart, the rains subside and the birds break forth in flight-winging joy. My heart fills with laughter, all thoughts are dispelled, and I am caught up in the joyful awareness of the birds' playful antics.

> They flitter and flutter and fly back and forth,
> > they feed on the feeder and land on the porch;
> of varieties many, can't count or keep track,
> > for never a moment, birds aplenty, we lack.

> Yellow dressed feathers with black striped wings,
> > the brown and red cardinal, her beauty she flings,
> the brilliant red male hopes him she will come to adore ~
> > we're surrounded by birds carrying colors galore.

> They perch and feed and push and displace,
> > flying from tree to hanger with a great deal of grace,
> into the tree limbs and hanging gray moss,
> > diving and dancing, now gone! What a loss!

> But they brighten the day with their rhythmic charades,
>   as they cluster and fluster in flashing parades;
> tree boughs and moss now alive with great motion,
>   then suddenly still, leaving soothing emotion.
>
> God gifts us with beauty wherever we are:
> We only need look at bird, tree, raindrop, or star.

Gifted with creation's reward of flighted beauty and the Spirit's lessons, my impatience is resolved. I relinquish to our divine Guide the time of our departure. The realization dawns that our "new way of riding" is not a gift received full-blown, but one into which we must live if we are to receive its fullness.

It appears I may have learned the lessons these five days were to teach me. The forecast reports the weather front moving past us today. Clear skies are promised. As we sit on the carport with our morning coffee in the very early pre-dawn, we listen to the wind and search the sky for a message.

> Cool breeze
> wings through the morning air,
> gentle breath
> of Spirit's love and care.
>
> The clouds
> cluster, then begin to break;
> moon glow
> bathes both cloud and earth.
>
> Moon glow and sunrise
> all darkness displace.
> Life fills
> with joy and God's loving grace.

Today we should be able to ride!

Journal, March 1st-10th

CREATION SPEAKS

We have enjoyed the love, companionship, and compassion of our family in rural Florida. The rain and predicted thunderstorms have held us here longer than we wished, but we are committed to traveling by Spirit's agenda, not our own. Today glorious sunshine bathes the morning. Our journey calls and we are ready and eager to respond.

> Ride forth, oh heart,
> let Spirit guide
> that into beauty we may ride.
>
> Created beauty,
> God's loving will.
> Our souls made fertile by His till.
>
> Let us receive
> what Gardener gifts
> so our lives become an image fit.

Leaving McAlpin, our ride winds through the rural farmland of north central Florida where the soil is sandy, trees hang heavy with Spanish moss, and cattle graze listlessly over the fields. We are glad when we finally reach the panhandle and turn south toward the Gulf of Mexico. Barrier Islands off shore, however, confine our view to the protected waters of bay and sound. For our overnight stay, we return to a place of happy memories we visited on a motorcycle trip more than a decade ago ~

Apalachicola. After these many years, we are delighted the same restaurant is still operating and once again we feast on delicious seafood. Returning to our motel, we reflect on this gentle day of transitioning into a new phase of our journey.

After a refreshing night's rest, we ride west. From shady woodlands, we emerge into the brilliant sunlight of the Gulf coast. The loveliness of the coastal scenes stirs within us awareness of the transforming power of God's presence in the created world.

> Soft rolling beach dunes,
> white glistening sands,
> aquamarine sea
> and dancing blue waves,
> purple flowers hidden
> in forest glen,
> all mellow our hearts
> and Love breaks in.

These tranquil beaches beg a time of contemplative rest and we are happy to comply. During our two-day stay in Pensacola Beach, we stroll the beach, dig our feet into the glimmering sands and the warm surf. Sunsets and sunrises paint radiant skies, and a spectacular thunderstorm offers a heavenly concert. As we watch from our balcony,

> clouds sweep and waves rise;
> orchestrated sounds
> thunder down from the skies;
> like crashing cymbals
> streaks of lightning flash;
> ice hail balls bounce
> and the gulls take flight.

This sojourn on the beaches of the Gulf helps establish the contemplative mode of our journey. Riding quiet back roads, we surrender ourselves completely to the joy of the ride and the beauty of the landscape. We hug the Florida coast and the southernmost boundary of Alabama. A delightful treat along this route is an open ferry ride, shared with a bevy of gulls perched along the raised gangplank. This trip across the rolling waters of the inlet to Mobile Bay lands us on Dauphin Island. A causeway carries us back to the mainland after which the road dips into Mississippi for our overnight stay in Pascagoula.

In the early morning, we ride out under the threat of ominous weather ahead. Severe thunderstorms and tornados are predicted to arrive sometime during the afternoon. We agree to watch the sky carefully; if it becomes threatening, we will pull off and find safe haven for the night. Our ride along the Gulf coast offers a smorgasbord view of the region's diverse creatures and plants:

> Gray heron standing in a creek bed
>   graces our day
>   with beauty fair.
> We ride for miles through barren wastes;
>   of flowers, we see
>   only a trace.
> Budding trees lift their arms to haze;
>   rose petals float
>   to sky in praise.
> Hanging white blossoms grace the trees;
>   their golden throats
>   a gift to please.
> Suddenly the egret's flash of white
>   calls spirits
>   back to Inner Light.
>
> God rides with us and speaks the Word
> Through plant, flower, tree, and bird.

Joying in the scene around us, we move slowly. We have little desire to increase the pace of our leisurely journey. Apparently, our divine Guide does not feel called upon to go along with our wishes; we begin to feel "nudges" that we are to move more quickly in this portion of our trip. The rising bank of dark clouds seems a signal to abandon less crowded back roads that would take us deep into the bayous of Louisiana. Following the leading we are being given, we turn north to connect with the interstate highway. Now we are riding directly toward the building storm.

We reach Baton Rouge under black and threatening skies. We must quickly find a room. That is not always easy because the air fresheners and cleaning agents used in motel rooms adversely impact Fred's allergies. Today we are fortunate and soon find a room offering no allergy problems. Moving rapidly, we unpack, lock, and cover the bike. As though a Divine hand has been holding it back, the storm breaks just as we complete all we need to do.

The fierce power of this storm is impressive. Safely in our room, we fix lunch and have our afternoon coffee. Fortunately, the tornados by-pass this area of Baton Rouge. We turn in for the night with the words of the psalmist singing in our hearts: "I will lie down and sleep in peace, for you alone, O Lord, make me dwell in safety" (Psalm 4:8).

Journal, March 10th-14th

The passing of last evening's horrendous storm has issued in a pristine blue sky as we wake this morning. Pondering the route we should take for today's ride, we feel we are being led to make this an interstate day rather than turning south through the bayous. In our gentle time along the coast, we were provided a foretaste of what our journey is to be. Now it appears we are to return to the "real" world. We trust we are hearing the message correctly. If not, we are sure "it will be made known."

Our interstate ride across Louisiana is not relaxing. Our alertness and awareness are consumed with the traffic rather than the beauty of nature. Pulling into a rest area as we enter Texas, we are offered a moment of tranquility. The Visitor's Center rests in the center of a natural bayou. Wandering on wooden plank walkways through this peaceful haven, we are sheltered from the nearby roar and race of the highway. The stop also provides a wake-up moment for what lies ahead. Fred mentions to the ranger that Texas must not comply with other states in having the exit marker indicative of the mile: "It certainly isn't 877 miles across Texas!" The ranger softly replies: "That's right! It is 879 miles across Texas!" We gasp as we remember friends' stories about the boredom of driving across Texas. We wonder what is really in store for us. Before riding off, we pose for photographs in the huge metal star that welcomes visitors to the vast expanse of the Lone Star State.

The ranger's statement during this short respite leaves us with lingering questions as we continue our highway ride. Eventually we enter the busy urban landscape of Beaumont, Texas. Our room tonight is immediately adjacent to Interstate 10 and the continuous sound of trucks rumbling along the highway assaults our sleep. Though I am hearing impaired and the noise does not annoy me as much as it does Fred, we both have a restless night. Waking early, we settle into silent prayer.

Hearts,
be still and in that place
let Spirit
enter and fill the space.
World's noise and clatter
set aside;
in God's Presence
now abide.

The thundering noise of teeming life
upon our spirits
is causing strife.

Spirit says:
"Set this aside; in our secret place

> now come and hide."
> The silence of that deep still Center
> quiets our souls.
> Peace now abides.

Our spirits calmed, we embark upon our day's interstate travel to our destination, Houston. Here we visit my aunt and uncle who are in ailing health. We also enjoy the companionship of friends whom we seldom see. During our stay in eastern Texas, we struggle with the busyness and noise of the city. After several days, we leave behind Houston's bustling metropolis and ride into the spaciousness of central Texas. We feel the landscape is opening its arms to welcome us "home." Is it possible this world is more "real" than the teaming urban life we have left behind? Serenity descends upon our spirits as we rejoice in the beauty of the open range.

> Yucca plants lift
> majestic white scepters.
> Green lacy leaves sprout
> on tree branches supple.
> Longhorn cattle graze
> on lush fertile pastures.
> Wildflowers blossom
> in scarlet, orange, purple.
>
> Divine beauty graces all the plains and the byways.
> Gifts of Love granted to all creation ~ Rejoice!

Our ride through this tranquil open range culminates in San Antonio. We share dinner and an evening with dear, long-time friends and then return to our motel for the night. Turning off the lights, however, does not turn off the ramblings of our minds. Sleep does not come easily. We are filled with anticipation as we contemplate the next phase of our journey.

When we wake, our spirits are impacted anew with our visceral response to leaving the urban areas and entering the open range. The Divine Spirit seemed to waft through our day with an intimation of what is to come. Intuitively, we sense that our "new way to ride" is releasing us into a new level of experience. Under the stars on the balcony of our motel, we have our morning coffee. Our hearts warm with a sense of Divine presence.

> Cup of Love ~
> overflows and spills upon
> high surrounding hills
> that we may ride into the Light,
> our lives and hearts
> by Love make right.
>
> Cup of Love ~
> filled to the brim with
> tears of compassion
> all spilled by Him
> that we may walk into that Sea
> so full of Love,
> and baptized be.
>
> Cup of Love ~
> now drunk with pain
> that peace
> upon the earth be lain
> that we may mingle unafraid
> and sprinkle Love ~
> free Gift, not paid.
>
> Cup of Love ~
> now emptied out:
> life poured upon earth's thirsty mouth
> that we may drink refreshing dews.
> Life of Love-spreading
> May we choose.

After a delicious breakfast, compliments of our motel, we leave behind our close human ties and watch familiar landscape recede into the distance. Now begins the major portion of our journey. We turn our bike southwest, along State Route 90, into the solitude of the West Texas desert. Because it is a quiet bike, our Gold Wing does not disturb the serenity of this virtually empty road. As we ride into the hundreds of miles of high desert, we are stunned into silence. Our eyes and spirits absorb the tranquility of this still, arid land. The aloneness engulfs us. We are intensely aware of the awesome challenge presented to any life form by this desolate terrain. Yet in a mysterious way, this vast silent landscape resonates with some deep spiritual longing within as we are touched by Transcendent Presence.

Reluctant to have this powerful experience come to a close, we must, however, find shelter for the night. We are entering the Armistad National Recreation Area through which runs the wild and scenic Rio Grande. The river is dammed to form an enormous lake. We end our day's journey in Del Rio, which rests on a high hill overlooking the lake. Here we hope to find a quiet, secluded motel. That is not given us! Instead, we find ourselves in a motel bustling with fishermen busily preparing their boats, equipment, and themselves for a fishing tournament to take place in the next couple of days. The lake is only a far distant vision beyond the greenery and flowering yucca plants inhabiting the sloping expanse below our motel.

We are being given two graphic lessons: our expectations will not necessarily be met along this ride, and the contemplative life is lived in community as well as in solitude. We laugh at this Divine disruption of our silent journey, enjoy chatting with the fishermen, and take a long walk. Finally, accepting with gratitude what has been given, we settle in for the night.

Journal, March 15th-20th

DESERT BLESSING

4

From Del Rio, the sparsely traveled Route 90 bridges the massive lake and provides a breathtaking view that soon fades into the distance behind us. Once again we enter the solitude of the West Texas high desert. The strange landscape and emptiness calls our spirits forth to float with the Spirit Wind just as the birds overhead glide, are lifted, and drift along on the lofty wind currents. I begin to understand why the ancients were called to the desert when they sought an intimate experience of God's presence.

> The sheer vastness of this space breaks spirits open
> to embrace the stillness and the solitude;
> the desert winds our souls soothe
> and beauty's peace holds sway.

The road gradually climbs in elevation and the long, listless flat desert begins to undulate into rolling hills. No gentle gradation into a mountain range, however; instead, there is a sudden scene change. We are surrounded by high mountains on either side, but each is separate ~

> rock rising above dry, crusty earth;
> steep-sided hills with crested domes;
> spirit figures cropped in stone;
> sharp peaks raised toward heaven;

> temple mounds embrace the land;
> on mesa's flat crown place of rest is given.

It feels as though the Creator has cupped hands around us in tender embrace, just as the mountains have embraced this high desert plain. In the vastness of this space, God is present and holding us. It is a transcendent moment! We must stop! The quietness, the profound stillness enters our spirits. We cannot speak! We can only be present to the wonder!

The penetrating silence brings inner stillness and calm. As we continue our ride, the mountains recede into the distance and our souls soar free once again. The love of Creator God, Whose presence fills this place, is impressed upon our spirits by the variety of life forms flourishing here:

> The empty plains tufted with weed
>   and cactus where cattle feed
>   seem so barren, naught could sustain.
>
> Yet life flourishes on in varied forms:
>   blood-red leaves drown the scepter
>   of yucca's white-flowered crown;
>   tiny wildflowers paint the landscape
>   in spreading fields of leafy gold;
>   one lone tree sparkles the land
>   with beauty-berry's magenta cheer.
>
> Myriad gifts of beauty strewn
> Spread nurturing Love upon our hearts.

In the midst of this desert landscape, the small town of Marathon suddenly appears on the scene and our eyes rest upon the historic Gage Hotel. We know this is the place we must stay for the night. Our room, furnished in Spanish style of the frontier era, opens onto a courtyard where climbing roses festoon the walls and the oasis' fertile soil buds forth blooms in colored array. A tiered fountain sprinkles musical sounds on the air. On the arbored patio, a rustic bench offers a contemplative space to pray and write. The sunset glows radiant as our spirits settle into this benevolent refuge.

> Night comes. Mud adobe shelters us,
> courtyard greets with radiant blooms,
> fountain anoints with flowing water,
> and canopy of stars blankets our rest.

In the early pre-dawn, we sit in the enclosure of our back courtyard. Looking into the black desert sky lavish with stars, we bow in humble adoration.

> God has brought us to this place
> to bless our lives
> with silent grace.
> Immensity of universe,
> the Word spoken in star-studded verse.
>
> Star-filled night sky speaks to us
> of eternity.
> Each glowing star
> of a Love once birthed
> in human form upon the earth.
>
> Flashing star breaks the darkness.
> A shining glow
> within souls awakes.
> Shooting star pours into hearts
> heavenly love, Holy Spirit's dove.

Following our star filled pre-dawn vigil and a hardy breakfast, we embark upon our day's journey. At this point, I begin carrying a pen and notepad in my jacket pocket because poetry is flowing even as we ride. When it is given, I take off my gloves, pull out pad and pen, lift my helmet shield and, bearing on my knee, scribble whatever is given. What is written on the road I later recopy into my journal. I am deeply grateful for this gift. Poetry seems the only medium through which to adequately express the musical praise of my heart evoked by the scenes and experiences that fill our days.

> Oh spirit soar, breathe in these gifts;
> lift our hearts in gratitude
> and songs of joy along our way.

We pause for a picnic lunch in Marfa, Texas. Later, at the visitor's center, we are told a captivating story:

> Of "Mystery Lights" over plains we hear,
> but only at night do they appear.
> Lonely town, Marfa, tells their story,
> God's gift to it of a unique glory.

Outside of town, we stop at the pull-off where people wait looking toward the distant mountains and hoping to glimpse the mystery lights. One legend says these lights are the flickering lantern carried by the ghost of an aged Native American man who wanders these hills and plains at night. Others have a more scientific explanation. Any explanation seems incidental as we stand beside our Wing and view the distant hills. The image of Light calling to my spirit through the darkness resonates with something deep within my soul.

As we ride further through this inspirited land, the whisperings of others who once populated this challenging terrain seem to float on the breeze and speak words of ancient wisdom through the scenes before us:

> Horses stand quiet in stately grace,
> their hearts longing to race across the plains
> and commune with native spirits long past
> whose lives were sealed and in disaster cast.
> Cared for by the Creator's hand,
> they all rode free upon this land.

> Their spirits rise and speak to me
> of caring for this land
> that its blessings still may flow.
> Why do our hearts learn, oh, so slow?
>
> All life is divinely linked on sacred earth in all its span;
> To avoid disaster's brink, we must work with creation's plan.

Though these are words of caution to all humankind, they become personal to us as we ride through this arid land. This is not a place to challenge nature. We are grateful to have a reliable motorcycle to carry us along and we are careful to bring a supply of water with us. The landscape paints a vivid picture of the impact of sun and drought and blistering wind. We are awed by the fortitude of those who lived upon this parched land. The fiery wind and sun must have seared their souls as it did the land around them. Confronted with the harshness of this beautiful landscape, I am cognizant of our vulnerability should something happen to our bike. Awareness of this lack of physical self-sufficiency awakens a spiritual counterpart, the need for reliance on the same divine Spark of the Great Spirit who offered sustenance and protection to those earliest desert dwellers. This land is winning our hearts while it burns into our souls.

> The land is dry,
> parched and thirsty from searing sun.
> Canyons are carved deep into the plain;
> wild horse herds gallop across the scene;
> wind-spouts lift dust by hand unseen;
> and hot, dry air assaults our faces.
>
> The fiery hand of Spirit Wind
> Blows burnishing over this land.

Near the close of our day's ride, as we leave behind this fiery landscape, our hearts receive an outpouring of the soothing oil of Divine grace.

> Out of this "valley of dry bones" we ride
> toward graced-filled mountains that call to us.
> We gaze high on a crested hill
> where stands a Cross ~ alone, stark, bare, still.
> From this lonely, hallowed sign, Love flows forth
> to soothe our spirits in cooling touch.

The landscape gradually yields the open desert to views that witness the controlling touch of human hands. Goat herds roam the hills and flood plains. Pecan groves surprise us along the roadside and somehow seem out of place. Less surprising are the miles and miles of irrigation ditches carrying life-giving water from the Rio Grande to expansive cultivated farms in the region. This modernized example of an ancient technique has allowed dry, thirsty land to become fruitful.

We are at the far end of the 879 miles of Texas, mileage even greater for us because of the deep southern dip we took to Del Rio. The trip, however, has not seemed long. In fact, our souls so resonated with this stark high desert we are sad to see our time there come to an end. Though the human touch becomes dominant as we enter El Paso, the inspiration of the desert landscape remains emblazoned upon our hearts.

> Our spirits have expanded so in mountain
> and high desert stillness.
> Creation's beauty imaged on souls,
> Spirit's gift our lives to bless.

Journal, March 21st-22nd

We stay in El Paso for a couple of days to catch up on the commonplace chores of this journey: mail, laundry, cleaning the bike, and repacking. This change of pace is refreshing; it allows a generative period during which our experiences root deeply in our spirits. I recall the Genesis story. Even the Creator took time out to rest, reflect, and exclaim: "It is good!" We rejoice in the bounteous gifts of creation so greatly enriching our lives.

Even the tamed and cultivated landscape of this desert metropolis offers an early morning star-filled sky evoking a hymn of joyous praise:

> As morning creeps
> across the night,
> sky from blackness
> glows midnight blue;
>
> Big Dipper glimmers,
> begins to dim,
> recedes
> into the eternal sphere.
>
> Shooting star streaks across the sky,
> God's gift of joy for those who see.
> City lights shimmer
> in prayer to Great Spirit
> for blessings
> upon humankind's endeavors.
>
> The heavens take on a radiant hue,
> spread beauty
> over the world
> like heavenly dew.

Leaving El Paso, we cringe at the thought of riding on the interstate only to be awe-struck as

> a highway unfurls on the desert sand,
>   melts into the landscape by color and form;
>   we ride on this vision as into a dream.
> Engineered beauty planned with an artist's eye,
> God's plan of Creation, his heart surely did espy.

This road is a graphic example of the ancient wisdom whispered on the wind: great beauty is the result when human creativity is in tune with creation's design. After a short distance on this lovely road, we turn onto a narrow byway. This barren road appears to be seldom traveled. There are no route markers, and the road stretches endlessly into the desert. To make sure we are taking the correct route, we question the driver of a truck stopped at the turn-off. Reassured by the driver's answer that this is the road we were told to travel,

> we ride out of the dream onto this tiny desert road;
>   passionate winds blow furious
>   across the plain.
> The scene stretches flat for miles before us:
> emptiness surrounds all that we see.

Enthralled by the scenes that unfold on this quiet back road, we ride in silence. I have been surprised to find how my soul responds to this desert land because I have always been drawn to the sea. Yet, we are both developing a great love for this beautiful, yet challenging, landscape.

This response to the arid scenes of desert is only one of the multiple changes we are beginning to notice in ourselves. We no longer think of miles to be covered; we are more present to the moment and the scene before us. Time is taking on a different quality. We feel free to drift, stop, or just be. We more easily relinquish our personal agendas to remain open to Spirit's guidance. Living into our "new way to ride" is reshaping our lives on many levels.

The flat stretches of the West Texas high desert won our hearts and helped us be more attentive to the spiritual lessons the landscape seeks to teach us. Now the barren desert of New Mexico unfolds before us. The perseverance of life forms adapting to the sparseness of this environment astounds us. We are challenged to examine our own lives.

Desert Blessing

> Birds are perched in tree branches bare,
>   their nests made of twigs,
>   their lives so spare.
>
> What can we part with, our abundance to pare down,
> that longing for God will be life's only care?

All day we ride in silent meditation on roads that twist and roll through soul-stirring landscape. As we enter Arizona, the desert land and mountains appear to live in cooperation with one another. Together they offer spectacular views that cause me to ponder what this desert/mountain landscape speaks to in my own life. As I reflect on the challenge of "letting go" we faced as we packed for this trip, I recall the words of spiritual author Wendy Wright: "Little is enough."** While the desert seeks to impress this Truth upon my spirit, it seems beyond my poor ability to grasp.

Yet, as I look at our Gold Wing, it seems to embody the same message. Our Wing is a stripped down model without fancy decorative painting, extra lights or chrome. Its essential function, carrying us safely and in comfort, is performed superbly. Our Wing helps us to hear the desert's message to free ourselves from non-essentials and live into a new awareness of the Divine intention for our lives. My heart listens! Its prayer drifts heavenward on the Spirit Wind:

> This naked land
> calls out to me
> strip bare my soul
> and so be free.
> It shows how little life requires
> to sustain the spirit
> be purified
> by Fire.
> The sacred plains
> and temple hills
> with divine Love my spirit fills.

A New Way to Ride–Listening and Following

I drink the wind
breathe the earth
bathe in the sun
to quench
my thirst for holy longings
which rise in prayer
to Creator God ~
present
everywhere.

Journal, March 23rd-24th

Interlude 5

In the intense experience of the desert, our spirits have embraced all they can hold for now. We need a period of quiet to give the seeds planted in our lives time to germinate. This is part of the rhythm of life to which we are not as attentive as we need to be. Sometimes it is hard to acknowledge this need because, when we are experiencing so much beauty, we want to push on, to grasp what lies ahead. Deep within, however, Spirit is telling us we need a time of repose to allow our experiences to take shape in our lives.

Leaving the spiritual inspiration of the natural desert, we enter the quiescent surroundings of the desert towns where we are led to places of more traditional forms of worship. A towering sixty-foot Celtic cross calls us up from Sierra Vista, Arizona, to Our Lady of The Sierras Shrine. Its cloistered setting high in the Huachuca Mountains provides a spectacular view of the desert valley far below. A chapel carved into the side of the mountain offers a place to linger for worship. Forming a backdrop behind the altar is a mural, painted by local artist Donna Ramaeker, of Jesus standing with outstretched arms. I am drawn into prayerful reflection upon its message:

> The Heart of Love
> housed in Thy breast
> now wrapped in thorns
> by sins of humankind
> who refuse

> to understand
> that God's plan
> is Love
> for life of peace
> and happiness.

> The Cross,
> empty now,
> rises from torn heart.
> Flame of Spirit
> makes souls bow
> who seek to receive
> the gift
> of Easter's promised
> new Life.

After a peaceful night's rest, we leave the tranquility of this mountain-embraced town and ride north on small lonely roads through rolling hills to the historic town of Tombstone, Arizona. Having visited here before, we stay only a short time and then continue to our destination, the Benedictine monastery in St. David, Arizona. As we enter the grounds of Holy Trinity Monastery, we are stilled to silence. Before us, silhouetted against the dark sky,

> a towering Cross stands in relief
> drawing to the Center
> lives lived by faith ~ not beliefs.

This soaring cross is identical to the one at Our Lady of The Sierras Shrine. Both crosses were commissioned and placed by the same man. When neighbors in his mountain community objected to this man's desire to build the Shrine, the huge cross was already commissioned. Thus the cross was generously donated to Holy Trinity Monastery. When permission was later received to build the Shrine, an identical cross was commissioned and placed high on the mountain at the Huachuca site.

Interlude

After listening to this intriguing story, we are welcomed to the monastery for several days of retreat in the guesthouse. This Sabbath time for rest, reading, reflection, and withdrawal from challenging "new growth" allows the experiences of our journey to take root in our spirits. As guests, we are blessed by joining the community in various aspects of their daily life.

> In monastery chapel,
> we gather in prayer.
> God's infinite Love fills this place
> and showers blessings
> upon each person's space.
> In psalms, hymns, and verse,
> our voices rise, as in unity of song
> the Creator we praise.
> Love unites us in this place
> into community
> blessed by Divine grace.

This monastery community is composed of a very diverse group of people: vowed religious, lay persons who have permanent homes here, others who come annually to help with the work and maintenance, and guests like ourselves. The Spirit bonding the community together is uniquely experienced when we gather for meals:

> "Greet all as Christ," their deep-seated rule,
>   is the warm hospitality
>   with which we are welcomed.
> In Benedictine Hall, our bodies are nourished
>   with food ~
>   both material and spiritual.
> The gift of delicious meals we partake
>   while music fills spirits with calm.
> Warmth of True Friend fills all with Love's glow.

We are not asked to join in the work times of the community. Instead, we are offered haven for our contemplative sojourn. The grounds provide various places to embrace the quiet time and deepen our spiritual lives. One such place utilizes remains of the pioneer heritage and features of the rustic desert setting to call forth spiritual images. We pause in turn beside an aged broken covered wagon, a collection of petrified logs, and a natural thorn bush as we follow this unique prayer-walk through

> Stations of the Cross
> that call to repentant hearts
> in all of the dark places
> Divine Love has sought.
> Painful,
> this crucifying of self-will's control;
> but only by this dying can lives be made whole.
> Even Jesus cried out not to die this dark death,
> But God in all tenderness said:
> "This death is the path to soul's victory."

Another place invites by an intricately carved oriental-red bridge arching over a pond. We are drawn through a sculptured adobe gate into

> the quiet Zen garden;
> a place for peaceful meditation.
> Deep ponds ~ artesian ~
> mirror Spirit's deep well:
> springs of Love and of Light
> which within each soul dwells.
> A bridge crosses over to walk
> and look deep for the beauty within.
> Around edges of the pond,
> iris radiate the glory of Life which God lends.

Here I spend much time in quiet reflection and writing. Other places on the grounds speak to our spirits in different ways. A walking path through low trees leads to a river where grasses and trees flourish along the banks: "...like a tree planted by streams of water...whose leaf will not wither" (Psalm 1:3). Most glorious is the open plain where stands a gnarled ancient tree stretching its twisted limbs in silhouette against the glowing red/gold/purple/rose of the sunset.

The clear, pre-dawn, star-saturated monastery sky offers the greatest nourishment to our spirits. As has been our practice for several years, we begin each day with this quiet time of being present to God. It is a time to stop listening to the ramblings of our own thoughts, to still our minds and hear the whisperings of Spirit's voice. Often it appears nothing is taking place, but over the years, as we sit in the silence day after day, week after week, month after month, we are changed. I cannot explain how this transformation happens. Spirit's work is hidden in mystery. At one point in our lives, we could not have imagined taking an extra hour early in the morning before our busy workday just to sit in silence and be present to the Divine. Once we committed to this time of contemplative prayer, however, it became essential to our day.

On this morning, our pre-dawn moments under the stars bring our sojourn at the monastery to a close. We move into our journey deeply centered in the experience of Divine presence.

> Night sky glows
> with stars' bright sparkle.
> Morning dews fall
> in gentle grace.
> Dawn's beauty glows
> with promise of sun.
>
> Spirit's gifts descend:
> calm hearts; quiet souls.
> Rejoicing, we travel!

Our hearts fill with gratitude for having been led to this place. Refreshed by this period of silent awareness, we ride north through the desert to Phoenix, Arizona. We travel most of this day on busy interstate highway. Fred must constantly be alert to traffic and I am keenly aware of the surge and flow of speeding vehicles.

Yet, the peacefulness gained in the solitude of the last few days shelters us throughout the day's journey.

Journal, March 25th-30th

We spend the next two days in Phoenix catching up on our mail and laundry. The latter is accomplished at a nearby Laundromat where we mingle with a few members of the local community, a convivial group of Hispanic families gathered here for the same task as ours. The men greet us with smiles, the children adopt us as instant grandparents, and the women welcome us into the ritual sorting, washing, drying, and folding of the Laundromat scene. We are grateful for this blessed gift of friendliness. When we return to our motel, Fred gives our Wing a well-deserved cool bath and checks it over to make sure all is ready to continue our travels. After our refreshing interlude, we are ready to be on our way once again.

During our short stay in Phoenix, the desert temperatures climb into the high 90's and low 100's. Summer heat has descended much earlier than anticipated. Our hope to spend time in Death Valley is shattered because the heat there is already extreme. Our desire and the path being laid out for us are not in concert. Such is the continuing challenge of our "new way to ride":

> I hear the words, "You are my beloved,"
> as a call to follow, whatever the road.
> That which the world counts of such value
> fades in importance, becomes but a shadow.

Thus we reluctantly relinquish our wish to visit Death Valley. *Listening and following* is still difficult when we receive a message opposing what we want to do. Reminding ourselves of our commitment to be *led* on this trip helps us embrace a different outlook. We set aside disappointment, open ourselves to expectant wonder, and follow this Divine "detour" westward.

In our morning quiet time before we leave Phoenix, I become aware of how strongly the desert has made its place in my heart. I am filled with longing for the quiet and beauty of the open desert sky. That scene is virtually obliterated by the incandescent urban sky at which I gaze through our motel window.

> One lone star calls out to me,
> but I must strain my neck to see
> for the world's lights all around
> seek to keep my spirit earthbound.
>
> Spirit's call of love is quiet and gentle,
> no noisy clatter or glaring mantle.
> Of Divine presence, I become aware.
> Shutting out earth's noise, I settle in prayer.

Cautious of the extreme mid-day desert heat, we take advantage of the early morning cool to ride the interstate highway across western Arizona to the California border. On this fast-paced trip, we are rewarded with stunning views of whole hillsides studded with

> Saguaro
> ~ sculptured artistry of Nature ~
> stands majestic
> upon the hills.
> Cactus arms
> droop in despair,
> angle wildly in clown glee,
> curve outward in greeting gesture,
> or reach toward heaven
> as through in prayer.
> Its aged body
> is torn and tattered
> by creatures
> seeking safe haven.
> Through nest-holes
> in saguaro's skin,
> birds
> wing out their songs

> of gratitude
> for sheltering home.
>
> For two hundred years,
> Bestowing beauty and tranquility upon the land,
> Saguaro stands.

A silent prayer fills my heart: "May I allow the message of Saguaro to find haven and take wings in my life."

The first town across the California border is Blythe, where we settle into a motel for a restful afternoon and evening. Pulling up our e-mail from home, we read that a couple in our faith community celebrated the birth of their second daughter on March 31. We rejoice with these Friends as they welcome this beautiful new creation into their family. We also celebrate the joy that this new baby and her older sister bring to our community.

> Miranda, Cassandra,
>   poetry in motion,
> bobbing curls and baby skin,
> steal our joyous hearts' devotion.
>
> Oh joy and wonder
>   of God's great Love,
> two beautiful parents,
> two darlings to love ~ gifts from above.
>
> Our community,
>   blessed,
> welcomes these small joys;
> holiness comes through a small child's kiss.
>
> The Kingdom comes
>   like a little child
> and warms cold hearts,
> for in these tiny lives
> God smiles.

Interlude

We depart from Blythe in the cool of early morning because we are once again riding interstate highway. Our precaution, however, is not necessary. Surprisingly, the heat is not a factor today. Instead,

> a strong, chill wind blows across the dry plain,
> bites into our spirit's claim
> of self-sufficiency and power:
> nature's force makes proud hearts cower.

The source of these chill winds gradually becomes visible as we near Palm Springs, a desert oasis surrounded by mountains. Through the open valley, pressed between the mountains, the wind rushes with a mighty blast and powers hundreds of windmills that churn out the electrical needs of this popular city. This spectacular sight of a valley full of windmills fascinates us. We are most moved, however, by the awareness that a clean natural power source has been realized through human creativity in cooperation with nature's bounty.

We welcome the cooler temperatures as we ride the ribbon of road through the valley to Palm Springs where we seek a place to stay for the night.

> Mountain sentinels, like heaven's gate,
> open to souls which in stillness wait.
> Snow-covered peaks draw hearts forward
> from soul-searing desert to cooling Divine waters.

> As we ride west, desert greens and starts to bloom:
> golden bunches, rose cactus plumes.
> Citrus groves give off heaven's fragrance,
> sweetness of Spirit's great expanse.

What a beautiful place ~ this desert oasis!

Journal, March 31st-April 2nd

DEATH VALLEY & LIFE

The Palm Springs oasis is bursting with glorious color as we arrive in the city; the buildings drip vines radiant with rose clusters. After securing a room, we walk into town for dinner at a charming, flower bedecked outdoor restaurant. Strolling back to the motel, we bask in the pleasantly warm temperatures and the beauty of a star sprinkled sky. Before retiring for the night, we sit under the stars for a time of quiet meditation and prayer.

We awaken in the morning excited over our planned ride into mountains north of the city to spend a few days exploring the Bear Lake region. At this juncture, however, our Spirit guide seems to take over our journey in a very direct way. During the night, the hot weather has turned cold and heavy snow has fallen in the mountains ~ not suitable for a motorcycle trip. Deigning this to be a Divine "detour" directing us from our chosen path, we surrender our wish for a mountain sojourn. We head for the southern California coast where we are sure it will be warm.

> My heart is merry, full of joy as we ride
> first toward mountains and then the coast.
> Radar shows a chilling cold front;
> Clouds circle in from off the sea.

San Diego is conspiring in the "detour" with drizzly rain and temperatures in the mid-fifties!

Hoping the weather will change, we stay on the coast for three days, one of which we spend at Sea World where we delight in the antics of God's creatures of sea and air. As our waiting period wears on, we seek to discern what message we are being given. The forecast indicates this weather pattern of chilling rain will continue all the way up the coast for the next week or more.

Gradually a clear message emerges: we are to change directions again! Apparently we are to make a full "about face" and turn back to the desert. Confused, wondering if we are hearing Spirit's message correctly, we nevertheless follow the guidance we feel is being given.

Leaving San Diego and riding east toward the desert, we gradually leave city behind and enter the southern mountains upon which hang low clouds. At first, the temperatures are in the sixties and riding is comfortable. As we climb in altitude, however, the sun begins to disappear and the shadowed green of the mountains becomes less inviting. When we reach 4000 feet, the clouds and we co-mingle; the chill settles in. Temperatures drop to the low forties ~ quite cold for riding a motorcycle. We stop beside the road to add sweaters, heavy outer riding pants, and winter gloves. Still, given the wind chill factor of a moving bike, the cold bites through our clothing.

Looking out from the mountain passes, we see far below the inviting green valley, sunny and lovely. This seems an image of what my spiritual life is often like; far in the distance I see the glorious sunshine of the peaceful valley while my spirit lies cloaked in the clouds of despair. Then Spirit's light breaks through my gloom just as sun now lights up the mountaintops. As the great stone boulders pick up the radiant warmth, we feel the sun chasing away the chill in our bodies.

As we drive onto the eastern slopes of the mountains, the wind intensifies and warms. The landscape changes radically: the chill green fades and is replaced by sandy soil, scrub bushes, and stones. The temperature rises. I welcome the scenes of high desert as though my spirit is longing for this land:

> God's message spoken is very blunt:
> "More work is needed! Desert it must be!"

Further along this mountainous road dark rust-red stone replaces the sandy soil of the hills. Huge boulders are piled one on top of the other. It is as though something has shaken the mountains and, while they remain whole, they are completely fragmented. The road winds through canyons traversing the rocky slopes. These shattered mountains summon from deep within painful images of brokenness I release to the Spirit Wind.

The shattered rock mountains gradually give way to a sturdier form that teems with the plant life of high desert. As we descend the mountain, we are awed by the rock layers of brown, tan, red, rust, purple, rose, gold, and white swirling and twisting to form abstract masterpieces painted by the brush strokes of the Master Artist. In silent wonder, we weave our way slowly through this gallery of natural artistry. This viewing, however, must quickly be assigned to memory. All that lies before us now is the blade of road that stretches across the bleak low desert scene.

Our ride culminates in a two-day holding pattern in the desert flatland of El Centro, California. We are plainly bewildered. What are we supposed to do? Are we just to sit and wait until the chilling temperatures along the coast subside?

Not receiving any clear answer to our questions, we make a side trip to Yuma, Arizona, for a Mexican dinner. Along the way, we are pulled from the main road by the magnetism of a sign that invites: "The Center of The World." A polished granite pyramid towers in the center of a cluster of condos and shops. Inside this dazzling monument is, sure enough, an embedded bronze plaque that gives the exact location as longitude 114 degrees, 45' 55.35" W, latitude 32 degrees 45' 1.38" N. The plaque further designates this spot as "The Official Center of the World." Surely, it is not to view this wonder that we have been drawn into one of "God's detours!"

After a delicious dinner in Yuma, we enjoy a pleasant ride along the southern fringes of the Imperial Sand Dunes Recreation Area. These massive sand hills gradually diminish until they become the flat desert plains of El Centro. We return to our waiting pattern.

> Pushed by the cold front from where we would be,
> Confusion reigns, like in the disciples' minds.

Our confusion and questioning are soon resolved in our morning time of listening prayer when we are surprised by one of Spirit's "nudges."

> Death Valley calls out symbolically ~
> "Ride desert road if you would be made whole."

We pull up the weather on the computer and discover the temperature in Death Valley is now in the seventies and eighties ~ perfect weather. Our desert sojourn is thankfully not to be in the flat windy stretches of El Centro, but in Death Valley.

With joyful hearts, we turn north. The straight concrete artery on which we ride cuts like a knife through the center of this vast expanse of dry terrain. Carrying debris of all kinds, the wind blasts across this desert plain and whips our bike with furious thrusts. We bend low to alleviate the wind resistance, but nature's power lets us know Who is really in charge. Controlling the motorcycle takes enormous concentration and the ride is tense. We are greatly relieved when the road finally turns east and the wind is at our back.

The journey then becomes serene as we ride through miles of wind-sculpted hills in the heart of the Imperial Sand Dunes Recreation Area. Here we take a break to delight in watching youngsters and their parents riding dune buggies over the spacious rolling sand hills. In viewing these vast stretches of undulating sand, we marvel at the beauty into which the Creator continuously shapes these ever changing mounds. We are enchanted as our gaze wanders over shaded ridges, sharp peaks, deep valleys, swirls and curls and sweeps sculpted into the slopes, and finally comes to rest upon the sparsely scattered groups of purple wildflowers braving life on these dry arid hills. Leaving behind this lovely place, we stop further along the twisting road to photograph the Chocolate Mountains ~ aptly named as their appearance resembles heaps of chocolate ice cream! Such a delightful repast would be quite welcomed at this point in our ride.

We complete our day's journey, and our long "detour," when we arrive once again in Blythe, California, from which we departed seven days earlier. We have come full circle, but disappointment and despair are not part of this scene. We have been given clear direction. Our hearts feel light and joyful and free!

Journal, April 3rd-8th

With a sense of assurance that the path has been chosen for us, yet not knowing what lies ahead, we continue our journey toward our given destination, Death Valley. The "why?" of this long detour is hidden in Mystery, but deep within there are stirrings of anticipation.

> Holy Week looms forth in my vision ~
> Jesus weeping tears from the mountain's view.
> Live into the pain was His decision.
> What is it I am being called to?
>
> Compassion ~ what God would have me learn!
> From desert's fire may courage flame.
> Dross of my heart may Holy Fire burn
> and Love be the fruit, not rejection's blame.
>
> May desert solitude and sparseness hold me
> in the tenderness of the divine Hand

and my life be stripped of all its coarseness.
May the blessed oil of Grace flow from this land.

Walk me, Spirit, through this shadow of death;
make love become my own condition.
"Accept the path set," God whispers.
"Tenderness brings reconciliation."

My heart shrinks from this call I'm given
to stand with one outside love's circle.
May compassion's tongue flame from heaven
and burn all barriers to welcoming's miracle.

As we ride into Death Valley, I experience a feeling I have never had before. It is occasioned by the impress of the surrounding mountains upon my spirit. The dry, barren mountains on either side of the road seem to rise higher and higher as the green slopes leading from the mountains to the road dip lower and lower. These verdant slopes gradually evolve into dry, petrified mud hills that seem to crumple under their own weight. It is as though the dryness and the heat has depleted their spirits and left their bodies folded in upon themselves like heaps of despairing flesh. My spirit feels the weight of this despair as we ride into this Valley of Death.

We ride deeper into the valley. The mountains press in upon us as though the earth is closing in to swallow us. The more deeply this feeling impacts my spirit, the more I empathize with how Jonah must have felt when swallowed by the whale. I begin to wonder if Death Valley is to be my time in the "belly of the whale," a time to let go of my resistance to allowing divine Love to birth in me the healing balm of compassion and reconciliation.

It is clear now that we were *led* on that long "detour" because we were to wait until the right time for us to be in Death Valley. To spend the end of Holy Week and Easter morning here in this valley of death is a true gift of Spirit we would have missed had we insisted upon our own agenda instead of allowing ourselves to be led. The unparalled beauty of Death Valley calls forth a deep response within our souls. Being present to the agony of these hills affords us a unique opportunity to live into the spiritual experience of these holy days.

> These great brooding mountains look down on me:
> I feel the weight
> of centuries of searing sun and burning thirst,
> their soul's anguish
> calls out for caress.
>
> Great gaping holes stare from their sides,
> empty hollows
> deep inside, cut through by floods to split apart
> great canyons
> carved into their hearts.
>
> I reverently bow before these suffering hills,
> icons of endurance,
> shaped by Spirit through centuries in the harshest
> of climes
> to endow the earth
> with heart-stilling beauty.

Spirit's tender touch reaches out from this tortured landscape to fill my heart with the message that Holy Week is meant to bring: that even in the most painful of life's experiences, God is present and working within us to bring forth new life, love, and beauty.

> My heart is so heavy I think it may break:
>   the pain of torn relations is causing its ache.
> The face of grief is painted in many colors.
>   Tears can divide, or reconcile,
>   with others.
>
> This great Valley of Death teaches us much about life,
>   that beauty may be born in the healing of strife.

> "God, send a star to brighten this darkness;
>   let hearts be filled with the love
>   of forgiveness."

Day is over. The crucifixion has happened. The tomb is sealed. Night has arrived. As is our custom on Good Friday, we have fasted all day. My body does not fare well when my blood sugar drops, so when the somber stillness of night falls, we walk to the camp store and share a dip of ice cream. Then we stroll across the yard, away from the noisy crowd, to stand beside the monstrously large form of "Old Dinah." This original steam engine replaced the twenty-mule-team wagons in hauling borax, "white gold," out of the Valley. Standing here is hardly a transcendent experience, but the one thing I have learned in my spiritual journey is one never knows when or in what ways God will break into our lives. Perhaps that is the reason why Benedictines say, "greet all as the Christ Spirit" moving among us. While we are in quiet reverie beside "Old Dinah," a young family, whose room in the motel is next to ours, joins us. They have seemingly adopted us this weekend and love to share their daily adventures. As they come bouncing into our presence, the young wife says: "This is 'Old Dinah' you know, like…(and then she begins to sing):

> Dinah won't you blow,
> Dinah won't you blow,
> Dinah won't you blow your
> horn…..orn…..orn………"

And on and on she sings! I am not ready for this! I want to stay caught up in the drama of this sad day.

Then in a flash of insight, awareness dawns! The message gets through! The divine Voice is telling me that, while sorrow and despair may cloud our vision, the deepest Truth of the spiritual life is Joy and Peace. With a grateful smile, we leave our new friends and retire for the night.

The tragically beautiful landscape of Death Valley offers much guidance for our journey along the spiritual path. Tortured centuries were required for earth's dynamic forces to produce these haunting scenes. Only through great perseverance were these enduring hills created. Daunting and treacherous terrain confronts us everywhere, most graphically on Devil's Golf Course where nature's powerful winds and rains shape crystallized salts into sharp spikes. This environment can test the limits of human endurance.

>Throughout this place, death seems to hold sway,
>>but if we look closely, life finds a way:
>>the waters of life lie close to the surface,
>>for those creatures who seek life, not death,
>>>as their purpose.

Incredibly, tiny life forms are birthed in the shallow bitter pools of Badwater's briny salt flats. From sun-baked mountains at Artist's Palette, inner beauty spills forth painting the seared hills with subtly hued minerals. And finally, the expansive larger vision of the Valley seen from the heights of Dante's View, births hope in the spirit of the journeyer:

>From adversity's cauldron such beauty is born.
>>"May my spirit not weep that my heart is so torn,
>but let pain bring spring rain of holy compassion,
>>that from sorrow of death, may
>>be born resurrection."

>The beauty of this Valley dwells deep in my spirit.
>>With the eyes of my soul,
>I feel its great passion radiating God's love.
>>Heart's sorrow glows white
>>with graced transformation.

Our third and final day in Death Valley is also the final day of Holy Week, much of which we spend in the shadowed presence of the painfully dry desert mountains. We are grateful to be making this ride on our Gold Wing. The silence of the Valley is not disturbed by the soft sound of our Wing. Being in the open, we are able to experience the feel of the landscape. The surrounding scenery envelops our bodies and spirits as our bike carries us along the great road through the Valley to the edge of the park. Solid granite hills and mudstone slopes close in on us like the walls of a tomb. The vast expanse of desert and rolling hills fills our souls with the quietness and numbness in which the disciples must have moved that day after the crucifixion ~ confused, depressed, wondering, and despairing.

When we ride through the last great divide, we look out on an immense playa across which we are to ride. There the water level is so close to the surface and the wind so strong it can blow stones, even 600-pound boulders, across the wet playa. This reality awes us as we cross over. On the other side, we drive a few more miles to arrive at a rustic inn where we are to spend the night. As the day draws to a close in the quietness of the Valley and the sun begins to set, our spirits are quieted with the same solemn sadness that must have settled upon the disciples as they entered the second night after the death of their dream.

We awake early on Easter morning to look out on the playa and across to the mountains while we wait for the dawn. As the sun's luminous platinum rays gradually pour over the mountaintops, the world comes alive. Our spirits embrace the wonder of that first Easter morn

> when the women crept silently
> to the tomb, to anoint their Lord,
> in the morning gloom.
>
> Watching the light rise over the hill,
> we envision that first Easter morn so still.
>
> Great stones across the playa are pushed
> by winds which come in a mighty thrust.

> The stone rolled away,
> from the mouth of the tomb by breath of God's Spirit,
> to bring life from death's womb.
>
> Mountains are silhouetted against morning sky;
> the darkness *we are* hides the Light from our eyes.
> Unbelieving, we do not recognize
> our Lord as He moves among us,
> both near and abroad.

Our hearts join the excitement and joy of that morning so long ago when the realization dawned that death does not have the final word. From the blood-soaked earth and darkness of despair, love, new life, new dreams rise victorious.

> The morning star gleams above the quiet hills,
> veiled in mist, in the morning still.
> Sky glows with promise
> hidden in mystery; the women's hearts know Truth
> that eyes cannot see.
>
> Watching the hills for morning's sunrise,
> we anticipate the glorious surprise.
> Desert morning glory opens its face to new day;
> trees flutter, creature life stirs
> as we wait for the dawn.
>
> The Valley fills with Light!
> Our hearts flood with Joy!
> Gethsemane's tears become resurrected Love!

What a blessing to be brought to this place for the holiest part of Holy Week. We will treasure these days in Death Valley as one of the most memorable parts of our journey.

Journal, April 10th-15th

A New Way to Ride–Listening and Following

    We leave our rustic dwelling in Death Valley shortly after the reverential alleluia of the Easter sunrise. Bathed in Easter joy, we ride through the mountains.

> Rock walls squeeze in
> like the mouth of the tomb.
> No boulder to close,
> they open to life
> and leave death's gloom.
> Emerging from the clasp
> of these sacred hills,
> my heart feels its freedom to fly
> where Spirit wills.
>
> Soul's work is done for this Holy Week session.
> May my heart keep growing in holy compassion.
>
> At crest of the mountain,
> Joshua trees bloom.
> I gaze over the valley
> and my spirit is awed.
> Down deep in my soul
> beauty rises
> from Death's Valley.
> I feel made whole!

    When we descend the mountain, the road releases us into the Owens Valley where our path stretches far into the distance along Route 395. As we travel,

> the great granite Sierras loom in mist beside us;
>   we ride in their shadow along the valley road.
> Artistically scattered, yucca plants blossom,
>   raise stately crowns across valley floor.
> Fanned by the wind of our moving Wing,
>   fragile red leaves dance in the breeze.

Leaving the flat plain of Owens Valley, the road winds through the soothing mountain passes of Sequoia National Forest and Greenhorn Mountains.

> Rivers flow rushing,
> the mountains become green,
> tiny blue flowers appear.
> Spirit's water of peace
> flows into my soul.
>
> The photos are printed, only upon heart;
> Soul painted with wonder, gift of Creator's art.

The sunlit beauty of our journey this day matches the overflowing of our Easter joy. When we arrive in Bakersfield, California, we relax into the evening quiet. Savoring the experiences of the last few days, our spirits are lulled into sleep.

Journal, April 15th

Blessed Interruption 7

Our spirits linger in the mountaintop experience of the last few days while fragrance from hundreds of colorful roses fills our motel room in Bakersfield. Surrounded by the rose-filled courtyard and immersed in memories, our minds confront us with a "real world" issue. Since the birth of our grandson on March 4, we have felt grandparent "nudges" urging us to break our trip and fly home for a few days. While we long to see and hold our new grandson, we are reluctant to leave our contemplative journey. Whether the "nudges" are of Divine or human origin, we seem unable to discern. The feeling that we are to fly home, however, is persistent. Receiving no distinct guidance, we finally decide we should go straight to San Francisco for a flight home. Comfortable with our decision, we turn in for the night.

Peace, however, does not grace my night's sleep. I am startled awake in the middle of the night with great anxiety over *our* decision. Apparently Spirit will not allow so easy a neglect of our commitment to being *led* on this journey. Finally, after two hours of wakefulness, I rise to sit on our patio under the stars and listen for guidance.

> Morning star shines
> in the darkness so bright.
> Its message:
> "Keep your thoughts centered in the Light."'
> It rises ever higher,

A New Way to Ride–Listening and Following

> in morning sky calling:
> "Let Light be the beacon to guide your eyes."

The message gradually becomes clear. We are not to ride directly to San Francisco, but instead are to take a leisurely route through the hills and along the majestic section of coastline from Cambria to Monterey. Apparently Spirit has gifts to bestow or lessons to be learned.

> As dawn brightens,
> star moves out in the distance.
> It draws us forth:
> "Follow me!" is its insistence.
> God leads our path forward
> if we are willing to listen.

This is one "detour" I welcome with joy! My mind and heart at peace I return to bed and sleep.

We agree this morning to follow the *leading* given during the night. We become especially grateful for this "star guidance" as we wind our way toward the coast along a twisting, dipping, wonderful motorcycle road through the mountains. Above us rise cathedral-like rocky spires. These lofty pinnacles lift our eyes heavenward. I am riveted with a powerful awareness of our relationship to the created world.

> Suddenly it all seems so clear ~
> what we have missed that was so near!
> It had appeared that on this ride
> we were hearing nature through our eyes.
> Yet now we realize a further truth:
> nature is gracing our days with her listening,
> a blessing enabling our hearts to start singing.
>
> As we ride through these stony cathedral hills,
> high rocky spires bid our hearts be still.
> Canyons deep within rising rock walls

bid our spirits' barrier walls to fall.
Creation is offering us a safe place
to pour forth our pain, joy, and fears.
Nature listens in love, in silence hears.

When the road plummets to a crossing over an arroyo, we stop.

Washes once flooded, now carry crystal clear streams.
Crossing the road, they sparkle in the sun's gleam.

Before we ride into this flow of rushing snow melt, we wait until a car coming from the other direction crosses so we know it is safe. As the wheels of our Wing are baptized,

we drop silent tears
to be carried away
in the fast moving waters.
Our hearts are blessed
by this gentle gift.

Eventually the road rounds a curve onto a flower-dressed cliff with a heart-stirring view of my long-time friend, the Sea. We pause!

Lovely orange flowers smile assurance to us.
Ocean's roar we hear far over the crest.
Invitation: "Come, sit before me and rest.
Let the quiet of my love-waves flow over your souls;
as I hear your stories, you become empty bowls.
For emptiness is required if God is to fill!"
We open our spirits to the rush of the waves;
we are filled with the joy of the Love that saves.

The last few yards of the road lead to secluded, windy pristine Jamarea Beach. This tranquil place feeds our spirits while we lunch, walk to the ocean, and toss bread to the sea gulls. As we begin the trip back to the main highway, we offer a prayer of gratitude for having met, while we were in Panamint Springs, the young woman motorcyclist who told us of this stunning ride. Divine guidance comes in varied ways!

On the rolling road leading from the beach, we come face to face with a landscape painted by the Master Artist: a lush green hillside is ablaze with brilliant golden daisies. In the midst of the field stands a single brown cow calmly grazing among the flowers. The tall yellow daisies paint a floral landscape against her tawny suede body. There is no place to stop for a photograph. The painting remains engraved only in our memories. No words are spoken, but Spirit receives the silent prayer singing in our hearts:

> Rolling green hills set a pastoral scene
> offering the peace of silence ~ accepting, serene.
> We wade through the wildflowers like the cow on the hill,
> and let beauty enfold us, our anxieties still.
> All creation accepts whatever we reveal;
> our words, thoughts, and feelings are held reverently
> in the great heart of Nature's love-listening.

As our bike takes the gentle roll of the hills and leans into the curves, we are filled with a silence only wonder can produce. Too soon the spell is broken. When we reach the main route along the coast, we enter a busy seaside metropolis sprawling its way to Santa Barbara. Here our overnight stay provides the opportunity to call a long-time friend.

Today our ride continues through highly developed sections of the coast, far from views of the ocean. Longing to regain touch with nature, we seek lodging for the night at Pismo Beach, California, in a beachfront motel. At twilight, we stroll near the surf of a gentle sea. High cliffs, which were formed by the eroding power of a stormy sea, form the backdrop for the flat sand beach. As the sun tucks its radiance beneath the covers of the horizon, the sky over the ocean glows with the blushed hues of sunset and spreads peace upon our spirits.

Journal, April 17th

Blessed Interruption

We ride northwest from Pismo Beach through scenic mountains to reach the renowned coastal section of Route 1 known as Big Sur. At the coast, however,

> fog drifts in; dampness covers the road.
> Anticipated beauty had filled our hearts,
> but riding coast road
> is not to be our direction.

Barely able to see the road ahead, we are not enticed to undertake this motorcycle trip of over a hundred miles. It appears that *our* plans are to be thwarted once again.

> We relinquish visions of high cliffs, seals so swift,
> waves crashing on stone and sun-sparkling surf.
> Centered in that place of being,
> we receive the Spirit's lead.

Slowly, we are learning to let go of our expectations and accept with gratitude whatever path we are given, even when it means forgoing a ride we really want to make. Consequently, we turn inland with waiting hearts to see what will emerge as Gift from this latest of "God's detours."

> Through fog-laden mountains,
> we ride toward the warm.
> Clouds disperse and give way
> to sun's dazzling light.
> Our hearts fill with cheer.
> Warmth floods our souls.
>
> Hills, vineyards, and valleys
> bathe us in beauty.
> Golden flowers
> are parables of a kind:
> "Be like blossoms of the field;

don't sow or reap,
but to Spirit yield."

Trusting in the Divine,
Our hearts are at rest.

Even the Wing seems to take on a glow under the touch of the sun's warmth. The lush produce fields, vineyards, and rolling green hills are so peaceful; yet, their beauty belies the meagerly-rewarded toil of the Mexican farm workers whose cause Cesar Chavez championed so diligently. This sudden awareness of how the back-breaking labor of others provides so much of what we take for granted is a sobering lesson as we follow the road leading through this lovely valley to Salinas, California. The sharp contrast between our lives and those of the field hands is branded into our consciousness by the luxurious new motel in which we spend the night. As we gaze through windows onto a field opulent with wildflowers, our hearts are humbled by this renewed recognition of our multitude of blessings.

Journal, April 16th-18th

This morning we continue through the valley until we enter the outlying suburbs of the San Francisco metropolitan area. Our spirits on this ride are less than sunlit because we know that arrival in San Francisco will bring to an abrupt halt this portion of our journey. As we contemplate the plan to fly home, our hearts are fraught with mixed emotions. We are thrilled to have the opportunity of meeting our new grandson and spending time with family. On the other hand, we find it difficult to leave a journey that feels like a holy pilgrimage.

The question with which we wrestle is, "How does this visit home fit into the pattern of *listening and following*?" We struggle to discern an answer. Slowly the realization dawns: "interruptions" are a part of the rhythm of both the spiritual journey and of life. If we demand things must work the way we want, these "intrusions" may seem like disasters. They may become blessings if received as part of the larger plan for our lives and lived into with peaceful acceptance and joy. Thus we arrive in San Mateo with a sense of assurance: this is part of the path along which we are being guided rather than a break from that path.

We are further reassured when we seek a way of storing our motorcycle and trailer while we fly home. Settled into a comfortable motel providing shuttle service to the airport, we ponder how to resolve this storage dilemma:

> We need to fly home and a place to store bike,
> someone's advice is what we would like.
> Look in *Gold Book*! This couple receives calls;
> we will dial them up and see what befalls.

The Gold Wing Road Riders Association's *Gold Book* lists riders who offer help at various levels. The name of a couple in San Mateo is listed to receive phone calls. We call. In a relatively short conversation, we explain our situation and ask if they can recommend a storage facility.

> "We'll store your bike," is their immediate reply,
> "and pick you up when you fly back."
> We go to lunch with these delightful two
> and know we are being gifted by the Eternal Who.
>
> There are people with whom God graces our lives.
> We never know who, it is always a surprise.

They are lively, gentle people at much the same stage in life as we are. Through this "blessed interruption," Spirit has provided the totally unexpected *gift* of new friendship. With our motorcycle, trailer, and possessions safely stored at their home, we place the keys in their hands. Returning to our motel, we feel extremely grateful as we prepare for our early morning flight and settle in for the night.

We arrive at the airport very early to await our flight. Though we are listed on a Triple 7 for "seats available" (courtesy of our flight attendant daughter), we will not know until ten minutes before flight time if we have seats. It is nearly time for the plane to leave and most people flying stand-by have already been called. I begin to feel this trip is ill-fated for us. Either no seats will be available or we will be seated in the very back of the plane. When we are finally called, we are given seats in the luxury first class section! That makes the trip home a special treat! I almost hear Spirit chuckling: "Judy, when will you learn to trust Me?"

On our first morning home, we sit on our deck and have coffee under the stars. It seems a moment out of time. No matter how often we fly, the transition from one place to another in such a short space of time, has an unreal, dreamlike quality for us. This transient "dream" brings a joyous reunion with some of our family.

> Being home ~ a very great blessing!
> The joy of grandchildren
> evokes cuddling and laughing!

Our tiny new grandson has such a peaceful personality. Holding this precious little bundle who feels of soft baby skin and smells of baby powder brings joy to both our grandparent hearts. His "older" sister, a two-year old toddler, makes sure she receives her share of the attention. Leading this delighted Gramma by hand to the playroom, she claims undivided attention for games and conversation. This happy day ends over dinner together in our favorite restaurant.

Today we travel to Charlottesville, Virginia, to visit another of our grandsons. This smiling not-quite-one-year-old charmer with sparkling eyes is a bundle of energy who has his grandparents breathless by the end of the day. Another delicious family dinner brings to a close these delightful two days with our youngest grandchildren and their parents.

Our time at home also offers the opportunity of worshipping with our faith community and experiencing the wonder of renewed relationships.

> Attendance at Meeting,
> where I felt estranged,
> prompts hugs from special friends.
> One dear friend,
> so filled with Light,
> helps anchor me
> and clear my sight.

Our spirits are warmed by this blessed time of reunion with family and friends. Now we are ready and anxious to return to our journey. With contented and happy hearts, we arrive at the airport and board the plane for California.

> Returning flight ~ joy takes over!
> Plane door closes,
> ramp disappears,
> peace floods our souls.
> Winging our way back to our goal
> of being with God
> on our ride through this land,
> we put all cares
> to rest in Divine hands.

Once we are in the air, our spirits soar. As the plane flies through virtually cloudless skies, we look down through the windows:

> Passing under our view ~ creation's beauty!
> The randomness
> of the natural world astounds:
> trees, canyons, deserts, snowy elevations.
> Great tidal wave of the Rockies
> draws the plains forth
> into a snow-crest of Spirit's voice.

A New Way to Ride–Listening and Following

Most breathtaking of all the scenes is this incredible view of the Rocky Mountains. The open land rises suddenly into mountains. This uplifting forms in stone the powerful image of a great tsunami, rising higher and higher, as though drawing water from the plain into a great mountain wave cresting and breaking to form the white snow-covered peaks of the mountain range. The image is imprinted indelibly upon my heart.

As we reach the western side of the mountains and near the coast, fog obscures the beauteous scenes below.

> Pilot announces,
> "Cleared to land!
> We don't have to hold!"
> The plane will be guided
> by instrument's hand.

We too must have faith in the "instruments" provided by the Divine to guide us as we ride into mystery.

When the plane arrives at the gate in San Francisco, we debark to be greeted by the friends who have graciously stored our motorcycle. Though we have known them only a week,

> like family, they welcome us "home,"
> not like someone who into their lives just roamed.
> With joy they offer us the freedom to stay
> and invite us to share their mountain get-away.
>
> How does one explain a choice so fortuitous ~
> a name from a book of someone to help us?
> Our explanation: "It is all in the plan!"
> And we accept with joy this gift from Divine hand.

We thank our friends for their generous offer of their in-town home for the evening, but express our great desire to return to our ride. We do accept with enthusiasm their kind invitation to join them at their mountain home for the weekend.

> Retrieving bike, we resume our ride!
> Spirit is Pilot,
> our path to guide.
> Across fog-laden Golden Gate bridge,
> we ride into beauty
> of sun-graced estate.
> Sparkling sea below ~ a marvel to view!
> We gaze from cliff heights
> at boulder-strewn, wave crashing
> ocean's delight.
> Riding the ribbon of road
> which skirts the coast,
> we breathe the air
> tasting of salt.
> Our hearts are resurrected
> from journey's abrupt halt.

After lunch in the quaint village of Stinson Beach, we continue our day's ride on the bluff that now edges a National Wildlife Preserve. Stunning vistas of sun-kissed cliffs and low-lying fog banks lingering far out over the ocean open us to a renewed awareness of the Creator's presence in all of life. Reluctantly, we decide that we must leave this spectacular road and seek shelter for the night. Thus we turn inland for a chilly ride through the mountains to Petaluma, California.

> Night settles gently on our returning.
> A quiet place of rest, bodies and spirits to refresh.

Journal, April 19th-26th

On our inland journey this morning, we spend the first part of the day in a medical facility to have a spot removed from Fred's forehead. This side trip provides the playful opportunity to visit Santa Rosa, the home of the creator of "Peanuts," Charles Schultz. Pausing in the town square, we are charmed by the larger than life statue of Charlie Brown and Snoopy.

A New Way to Ride–Listening and Following

Leaving the quiet of Santa Rosa, we soon join the noisy, traffic congested, interstate highway for a taxing ride to the mountains. In this distracting milieu, bouncing along over the tar-repaired cracks on the cement highway, Spirit gifts me with the poem verses expressing so well our gratitude for the loving welcome of these new friends.

Upon our arrival at their mountain home, we are greeted warmly and welcomed into their larger circle of local friends. In addition to warm human companionship, their home's sylvan setting provides a time of quiet and rest. Overlooking a stream on the hill behind the house, their children have cleared a forested area to honor their recently deceased grandfather. "Fred's Place" holds a bench for remembering and meditating. I spend much quiet prayer time there and through my journaling, it becomes a place where God's healing balm caresses my spirit and brings a sense of peace.

> This gentle place nestled
>   among the trees
>   to mourn and grieve
>   sets hearts at ease.
>   In memory of one loved so dear,
>   who is in body no longer near;
>   a place of seeing,
>   of spirit only,
>   our hearts so lonely.
>
> So upon this bench we sit
>   and let the pain our spirits wrench.
>
> Towering ponderosa pines surround,
>   tiny green plants abound,
>   moss-covered boulders lie still,
>   sun-sprinkled treetops break spirit's chill;
>   a place apart
>   for memories to rise:

        we lift eyes to the sky.
We are warmed by the sun of Spirit's touch
and remember a love that filled our lives so much.

In stillness, our hearts retreat
    to that quiet space
    where lies healing Grace.
    Pains can be carried there
    and placed upon the altar bare,
    for we are held in God's loving care
    and made whole.
Through this dark night, Spirit enfolds our being.
We experience the Presence; no need for seeing.

After a joyful two-day visit, we say good-bye to our friends. Tucking away beautiful memories in our hearts, we ride through the picturesque Sacramento Valley toward the coast. We are deeply thankful for the surprise gifts of places and people we have received by following the *whisperings* of Spirit into this "blessed interruption."

Journal, April 27th-29th

CREATION'S HEALING LOVE

The memory of our visit with new friends lingers in our hearts as we travel through the pastoral scenery of the Sacramento Valley. Riding west, we are lured from our rendezvous with the coast by the call of a virgin Redwood grove. Responding to this call, we stay overnight in Ukiah, California, the nearest town to the Montgomery Grove.

As we leave Ukiah today, our hope is to fulfill Fred's dream to visit the "Tallest Redwood." Filled with hushed anticipation, we follow a twisty, roller-coaster road and gaze over sweeping vistas beyond the valleys to the distant Sierras and other mountain ranges. The hills are picturesquely manicured by the grazing of cattle and horses meandering across the landscape. The road parallels a gurgling mountain stream and descends into the shelter of the Redwoods. Feasting our eyes on the surrounding scene, we are totally unaware of having passed the entrance to the Grove until we begin to exit the Redwood forest. After a difficult u-turn on this twisting road, we become more attentive and soon we pull into the parking area.

The path into the Grove leads three-tenths of a mile to a circular cluster of trees. In the center rises the magnificent "Tallest Redwood" ~ 367.5 feet ~ awarded that distinction when its predecessor lost ten feet from its top during a storm. As we stand in the Montgomery Grove, we experience the unique sacredness that seems to enfold Redwood groves. The cathedral stillness of this particular Redwood grove touches us powerfully and bids us be silent before the Presence. Under the shelter of this Tallest Redwood, we sit motionless in prayerful quiet. From deep within stirs this hymn of praise:

> O sacred space
> among these templed spires
> ~ Redwood trees.
> Light breaks through with sun's embrace;
> God speaks in silence
> our hearts to grace.
>
> This circled "ark of covenant"
> between humankind and creation
> is lent to us only for a time.
> Holy quiet. Peace sublime.
>
> Solidly rooted in rich soil,
> stretching
> toward Heaven's whispered call.
> Majestic bodies of wooded girth
> within our spirits
> wonder births.
>
> Sun gleams
> through fragile branches
> of tree so tall.
> Its massive trunk
> dwarfs human size;
> our touch is gifted
> with its spirit's prize.
>
> The oldest,
> born near time of The Star,
> peacefully watches from afar
> our human struggle
> to conquer earth;

>   to live in harmony
>   humankind must learn
>
>   Through time, fire, storm, and saw,
>   Their gnarled roots and towering limbs
>   speak their truth:
>   "All creation, one with Him."

Prayerfully, we leave the chapel of the Redwood grove and follow the rolling road through Mendocino State Park toward the coast. Arriving in Mendocino, we are once again wrapped in the ebullient embrace of the ocean's beauty. Riding through the streets of this quaint village, our eyes rest on a little white clapboard house. Adirondack chairs adorn the porch. Redwood benches grace a garden profuse with flowers and roses. This lovely bed-and-breakfast cottage, the Sea Gull Inn, overlooks horseshoe shaped cliffs. Far below white-crested waves roll into the cove formed by these cliffs. We secure a room offering a view of the ocean through lacy, white ruffled curtains. Another window provides a close-up portrait of the multi-blossomed blooms of white hydrangea bushes. Gifts of life ~ redwood trees, the sea, and flowers ~ surrender us to peaceful rest.

With so much natural beauty to enjoy, we long to have our early morning coffee while sitting out in the pre-dawn dark. As is the case, however, in most places where we stay, lights surround the building. We understand the owner's concern for the safety of her guests and the security of her property. The sad question of my heart is, "Why is there the need for such concern, even in a seemingly peaceful little village like this?" It is a question with which my own heart must wrestle and one which posits a larger question:

>   Why is it people need so much of their light
>   when God provides so much beauty at night?
>   We long to gaze

A New Way to Ride–Listening and Following

    into the dark sky
    and be bathed in the beauty of starlight.

    Humankind's light seeks to hush the dark:
    fear of shadows stalks the heart.

It is difficult to find a spot where we can sit in darkness and listen to the sound of the sea.

On a lower step of the Inn is a sheltered place where we are not assaulted by artificial light. Sitting there, we are gentled into the day.

    Twinkle of stars
    and glow of moon
    shower earth with a loveliness that enlightens the night.
    God's presence we feel in the dark stillness;
    our spirits are showered with the light of Grace.

    Dawn rolls in like a luminous sea,
    washes away the stars' sparkling light.
    As black of night turns
    to morn's deep blue.
    Creator's love enters our hearts anew.

    The sound of the dove falls on our ears,
    joins wave sounds and breezes near.
    As the ocean crashes
    over boulders on shore,
    the sounds of dawn's peace splash radiant Love

Before leaving Mendocino, we walk through fields of wildflowers on a rocky path winding to the edge of the cliffs. There we marvel at the sight of waves rolling and tumbling over one another in a race toward the sandy beach far below. The peacefulness of the scene obscures a secret hidden in the sculpted sides of the cliffs ~ the danger of a stormy sea or a rogue wave sweeping us off this bluff to be forever joined to the sea. The reality that such an occurrence can and does happen is sobering. Today, however, we bask in glorious sunshine and the sight of a gentle sea.

Leaving our cottage, the road circles the village along the edge of the cliffs. We say good-bye to lovely Mendocino and head north on the famed Route 1 highway as it winds its way along the coast. The spectacular view of the ocean crashing against the sea-stacks and bouncing on the shore imprints its message upon our spirits.

> God sculpts gardens of the sea:
> > gigantic boulders;
> > turquoise waters
> > dressed in shawl of lacy seaweed,
> > crocheted edges
> > layered white with foamy surf
> > upon shore's black sand.
>
> Sea of God's Love sculpts our life:
> > its jagged sins,
> > all its strife
> > washed over with green sea of Love;
> > black sand darkness
> > in silent cove
> > cleansed with surf of forgiveness.

As breathtaking as the view is, however, we cannot ignore the ferocious winds blowing across the tops of the cliffs. We must acknowledge the effect it could have if we do not respect its presence. There is no doubt which of us is the more powerful!

> From the sea, winds blow strong:
> > blustery gusts
> > force recognition;
> > bike must lean into this wind.
> > Holy gale
> > sweeps across spirits' landscape,

> bows hearts in humility,
> empowers lives.

Intense concentration is required to hold the bike steady in this sideward sweep of wind. Fred is much relieved when the road turns inland from the coast to become wedded to Route 101, The Redwood Highway.

> In quietness of mountain pass
> towering Redwoods
> guide eyes
> toward heaven's stillness.
> Templed nature
> calms wind-blown spirits,
> enfolds us in timeless Presence,
> indwelling creation.

We leave Route 101 for a side trip to Leggett, California, for a visit to the original Drive-through Redwood. The Chandelier Tree is 2400 years old, 315 feet high and 21 feet in diameter. Seeing our Wing slowly move through this massive tree, we are again reminded of the gifts that result from the merger of human imagination and Divine design. We enjoy picture taking and a tour of the gift shop where we purchase small bowls turned from the burls of redwood trees. Artistic grain forms the character of these bowls, offering an example of the Creator's attention to beauty in minute detail.

With a final pause to stand once again in the presence of the massive Chandelier Tree, we resume our ride north to Garberville, California. In this bustling tourist town, we manage to find accommodations tucked away from the hustle and lights of the main thoroughfare. The view from our window is of a grove of trees, among which stands a towering redwood. The quiet retreat setting of this motel provides much needed calm because we are filled with anticipation about what tomorrow has in store for us.

Journal, April 29th-May 1st

In the still darkness of our pre-dawn meditation time, we feel a sense of awe as we recall what led us to plan today's ride. The California guidebook, which we peruse from time to time, highlights places of interest a traveler might wish to visit. Some of these places attract us, some seem to have no appeal for us, and others seem to leap off the page calling out to our spirits. When the latter happens, we take note for as the prophet Isaiah says: "Your ears will hear a Voice behind you saying, 'This is the way; walk in it'" (Isaiah 30:21). The Voice spoke when we read about the secluded fishing village of Shelter Cove.

Mario Machi established Shelter Cove after serving in World War II. During the war, Machi received the Bronze Star, survived the Bataan Death March and three years of Japanese imprisonment. Returning to California after the war, Machi founded Shelter Cove and carried out numerous courageous ocean rescues. The bronze statue in the village acclaims him

> Hero in war! Hero in peace!
> Respected teacher, author, and historian
> The Spirit of Shelter Cove

We seem drawn irresistibly to this little fishing village. We are not sure why, as it is so far from our path, but it is calling out to us. As we leave Garberville to make our way along the only road leading to this isolated village, we are swept up in a spirit of fervent, even reverent, expectation.

> Shelter Cove ~ a whispered name
>   for days has lingered
>   to us singing a longing,
>   a cry of soul
>   a need aborning.
> Spirit's ways we do not understand.
>   God plants a seed
>   a thought
>   a plan.

A New Way to Ride–Listening and Following

> We know within our inner being
> We must follow without seeing.

We leave the major road for the winding secondary road through the back country settlements of Redway and Briceland. Both towns seem fairly typical of small mountain communities, each with a post office and a corner store/filling station. Spreading out from the store/post office hubs are home sites scattered over the mountainside and in the woods. We enjoy the familiarity of these scenes as we slowly lean our bike into the curves and twists of this road through pastoral land. Then suddenly, without warning, the road dips and opens into the profound silence of a Redwood grove:

> Towering trees form temple spires.
>   I cry out!
>   My heart stops still
>   ripped from its shell
>   drawn to deep well
>   of Redwood cathedral.
> In this virgin forest stillness,
>   pain and beauty join
>   in peace.
>   Calmness settles
>   on my being ~
>   turmoils cease.
> In this sacred quiet,
>   God is present
>   in my life!
> This Redwood temple houses Spirit's being;
> We stand on holy ground.

I surrender completely to this sacred moment. I know that I am being made ready ~ for what, I do not know.

> My soul prepared, we leave this place
>   to ride on

> be graced with whatever
> God has planned.
> We simply follow the Guiding hand.

As the Wing, in hushed silence, glides from beneath the shaded nave of this sacred Redwood grove, the road begins to climb; it twists and turns through the evergreen forest. At 2500 feet, we round a curve and catch the first heart-stirring glimpse of Shelter Cove.

> From two thousand feet on mountain top,
>   through graceful trees,
>   we see the sea.
>   Beauty untold,
>   it rolls before us.
> We descend
>   to ride its shore,
>   feel its spray,
>   hear its roar.
> Great rocks jut out far from the shore.
>   Sea cares not,
>   it waves and crests,
>   crashes high,
>   sends white plumes of beauty
>   toward the sky.

Entering the village, we ride through the few streets looking for a place to secure a room. It quickly becomes obvious where we are meant to stay. There is one small motor inn sitting a few yards back from the edge of the cliff and facing the sea. It is not a busy time for the inn, so there are vacancies. The manager is accompanied everywhere by a handsome dog who looks much like a wolf; as it turns out, he is mostly wolf, but very friendly and gentle. Beautifully groomed, he is truly one of the most handsome dogs I have ever seen.

We ask for two nights and quickly run up to our suite to see what it is like. After settling in, we go out for quiet time on our balcony and watch the continuous performance of the ocean breaking on the gigantic boulders edging the shoreline. With no understanding as to why, I am brought to tears by the beauty and gift of this place. Here, we are very aware, we must stay awhile. We return to the manager's office and tell him, "We have a problem." When he asks what it is, we respond that two nights simply are not enough; we need three nights at least. He says that is fine, but we cannot stay longer because he is booked solid for the weekend. Once again, "little is enough." Spirit has provided the time needed.

We return to our balcony and our spirits merge into the scene of the azure sea as it rolls toward us. As the tide recedes revealing huge rocks further out in the ocean, I enter fully into the wonder of the waves breaking, in explosive splendor, over those ominous black boulders. And suddenly I know! I know why I have been brought to this place.

> I hear the sound of sea cry out,
> "My dear child,
> this is my Love
> which blots out
> the dark rocks
> within your life
> and covers with beauty
> all their blight."

My whole being is flooded with the only Love that heals and frees ~ that of The One. In this moment, I am overwhelmed with the awareness that I am the beloved child of God. Everything else pales, diminishes, becomes insignificant. As I watch the sea, grace flows in, forgiveness abounds, and I desire only to love as I am Loved. Truly Spirit's healing touch!

Tears of peace, love, joy, compassion, forgiveness, and humility roll down my face as my spirit is harbored in this transforming moment. In the quiet stillness of the sunset's waning glory, my heart whispers a thankful prayer for this inpouring of Love.

> This glorious cove shelters us,
>   offers beauty,
>   refreshes hearts.
> I feel so loved by the Eternal One
> My heart overflows with gratitude.
>
> May my life I surrender,
> Holy Love be my only guide;
> Let Spirit fill to make anew,
> And in my life, peace abide.

The days at Shelter Cove are hallowed days! We are baptized in the ineffable view of the ocean crashing over huge boulders in the sea. We walk the black sand beaches and venture forth on the jutting promontories along the coast. We watch the tides shoot towering flumes into the sky and joy in the birds' feasting dances when the tide recedes. As we gaze in wonder, our hearts are melted into the vivid colors of the sunset sky mirrored radiantly on the sea.

> Birds dart and dive as they gather day's food;
>   one sits on the rocks to catch
>   the sea's mood.
> Other birds perch on stones high above sea,
>   the sunset's beauty absorbing,
>   as do we.
>
> Evening stars set in twilight's blue pillow,
>   while morning stars twinkle from
>   darkness of night.
> Shooting stars race across the scene
>   and hearts reflect glow
>   of moon's beam.

Sunlight dancing upon the waves
calls us to watch how
we behave.
All of this beauty touches our spirits,
reminds us to be thankful
for much.

Misty mountains offer promise of more,
of wonder and beauty held
yet in store.
This quiet haven with its tall cliffs
has brought to our spirits
a magnum shift.

Shelter Cove,
beautiful place,
fashioned by God's loving grace,
etched within memory's treasure:
tranquility and peace
without measure.

Our time in this grace-filled place comes to a close. The words of Isaiah 60:5 sing in our hearts as we ride:

"Then you will look and be radiant,
Your heart will throb and swell with joy;
The wealth of the seas will be brought to you."

Journal, May 2nd-5th

COVENANT

The worshipful aura of Shelter Cove surrounds us. Fearful of breaking its spell as we leave, we ride in silence. We reach the top of the mountain and pause for one last longing look.

Quietly we turn away and continue through "The Lost Coast" until the Wing's tires touch Route 101 heading north. For most of the day we skirt the Humboldt Redwoods State Park. In grassy fields along the road, we gaze at herds of Roosevelt Elk grazing, resting, or lifting their heads to return our curious looks. In other places along this Redwood Highway, the road winds through sections of redwood groves. We take the ride through "The Avenue of the Giants" where the immense size of these trees witness to the appropriateness of that name. While the size of these "Giants" inspires awe, our spirits most delight in the close up view of the huge burls bulging from their sides that form platforms graced with moss, clover, and fern. The protection of these delicate plants by the mighty redwoods is an enduring example of the interdependence of the natural world.

Desirous of a more intimate contact with these noble trees, we turn onto a side road winding deep into the forest. We move slowly and submerge ourselves in the sensory presence of this magical woodland. The road becomes steeper and steeper as we move more deeply into the forest. The smell of an overheating engine breaks through our meditative mood. This snail-like pace on such a steep incline is too great a strain for our Gold Wing. We pause to let the bike cool down and are provided a time of holy calm in the moist serenity of this virgin wood. Our slow descent to the main highway allows us to ease back into the bright sunlight of the pathway north. By day's end, we arrive in Eureka, California, on the edge of Humboldt Bay National Wildlife Refuge.

After a restful night, we indulge in a delightful brunch of smoked salmon omelet served up at a restaurant in Arcata where we watched the wind whipping the bay waters into whitecaps. From Arcata, the road north traverses chapeled redwood groves and touches points along the sparkling sea. By late afternoon, we pull into a viewing area situated on a high cliff from which we look down on the huge horseshoe shaped cove that gives name to Crescent City where we will spend the night. As we look at the scene below us, we do not find it difficult to envision the 1964 tsunami rolling onto this flat beach and devastating the landscape. Now, however, the cove is one of tranquil beauty.

Our overnight lodging is situated right on the beach along the inner shore of the crescent. Scattered over this beach are hundreds of sand dollars deposited on the shore by the rolling waves. Under a dark sky filled with floating, misty clouds, we sit out on our motel deck in the early morning. A full moon bathes the sea with shimmering light and so illuminates the night sky that we see only three stars. While the lighthouse beacons the danger of the rocky point,

> the fog horn's mournful cry calls warning
> to guide seamen in safety
> through hazardous shoals.
>
> The sea is so vast, all else it humbles;
> on its dark expanse, arrogance crumbles.
>
> The fog horn calls through the mist,
> and buoy bell signals that path not be missed.
> The seafarer knows the voice from the shore,
> listens carefully, for to secure anchorage it lures.

Covenant

> The Divine Fog Horn calls over the sea of our lives.
> To harbor's safety we are guided
> By Spirit's voice which within us resides.

After a quiet walk along a beach glowing with the rose luster of dawn, we prepare to bid farewell to Crescent City and California. For thirty-two days of our journey, this beautiful state has provided wonderful experiences of growth, awareness of God's presence and love, and sanctuaries of solitude and peace.

As we enter Oregon's southern coast, the scenery seems more wild and untamed, yet extraordinarily beautiful.

> Oregon greets us
> with chill, blustery winds.
> Towering forest green of
> aspen, cedar, spruce
> drop lacy-shadowed stillness
> enfolding our ride.

At first the forests march down to the edge of the rocky coast. Further along logging has decimated the primeval forests. The few trees lining the road block views of the coast, but fail to cover the vast acres of

> clear-cuts calling forth
> compassion from within.

Our hearts rejoice as we enter areas where the scarred earth is yielding stands of new growth woodland and panoramic views of coastal splendor.

> Whitecaps break
> on aquamarine sea;
> fog bank poises
> low over distant horizon;
> massive monoliths rise
> from ocean's embrace,

> stone heads lifted
> in praise of Creator.
>
> Sun banishes the clouds beginning to roll in.
> We accept all as blessing and ride in joy.

Arriving in Coos Bay, Oregon, we settle for the night in a lovely motel. Our balcony overlooks the river and flowering bushes below. The morning vista from this same balcony offers a set of sharply defined contrasting scenes:

> I sit on my balcony and what do I see
> in all of the scene set before me?
> Across the river, the lights of gravel industry,
> further on bright neon shouts glaringly.
> Hotel sign greets with "$27 Single;" that's fine!
> Traffic roars across bridge: "Must get to work on time!"
>
> The scene changes and mist covers the trees;
> the sky turns from black-blue to gray
> in the morning breeze.
> The quiet river, a mirror, reflects the shore:
> upside down trees, grass, flowers, and more.
> Flock of geese honk by in morning flight,
> and flower petals cover the ground in my sight.
> A fish jumps out of the looking-glass river.
> Ripples of joy spread forth over its surface.

Given our penchant for sitting in darkness under the stars for our time to be with God, I find these morning scenes distracting until a question arises in the silence.

> As the sky is painted with dawn's lovely rose
> And the neon lights continue to glow,
> I am asked to ponder: "In which scene is God clothed?"
>
> For this is the challenge of my spiritual life,
> to realize God's presence, whatever my plight:

> in beauty, in friends, in joy and celebration,
> in ugliness, enemies, pain, and separation.
> When my cup empties, Spirit's peace fills.
> Awareness of God's presence is wondrous surprise.

As we prepare to leave Coos Bay, practical considerations take over our thoughts. We must take time to care for our motorcycle. Our Gold Wing has performed like a champion on this trip, never once detracting from our journey by needing attention ~ with the exception, of course, of a periodic fuel refill. At the present moment the Wing is crying out for an oil change and the need seems pressing. Unfortunately, the biking season here in the Northwest is just beginning and mechanics are swamped with work. When we call the Honda shop, the mechanic says that he simply cannot fit us in, but we may use his shop and tools if we can change the oil ourselves,. Accepting this gracious offer, we spend a very cold morning in an open garage caring for the Wing's need. Though we are chilled through by the time Fred completes the task, we are grateful for the gift of this kind mechanic. Happy once more, the Wing receives our bodies and the three of us continue our journey north.

> We celebrate beauty along the way;
> God is opening our lives to it each day.
> Beauty is given in many forms:
>> in sunshine
>> in storm
>> in scent of pine;
>> in waves crashing
>> and birds dashing.
> Wonder in our hearts is easily born.
>
> As we ride in the wind
>> and feast on food from the sea,
>> all of life blends
>> into peace and serenity.
> God's presence we feel in all around:
> Divine blessings flow into life without bound.

A New Way to Ride–Listening and Following

Our lovely coastal ride this afternoon brings us to Florence, Oregon, for an overnight stay. When we continue our journey north along the coast, our attention is gripped by ocean vistas of

>glorious turquoise waters
>crashing on monolithic sea-stacks;
>volcanic lava-flows,
>frozen as they touch the sea and
>creating coastal landforms of mystery:
>dark fingered configurations with inlets and holes
>where waves crash, water-spouts flume, and tidal pools form.

We park the Wing to hike a trail winding among these lava-flows. The waterspouts blowing high into the air and the azure sea dancing in foaming splendor into the inlets send mist floating on the breeze to caress our faces.

Wondering what more beauty our hearts can hold, we mount our Wing and ride further along the coast. The road dips from the high cliffs to curve along the beaches and allows us to breathe the sea air and feel the saltiness on our skin. Then the road climbs again to high cliffs where

>a wondrous new gift unfolds:
>sea lions bask in the sun, after winter's cold,
>their cadenced sounds rising from the rocks below
>the simple joys of community show.

We take time here at the Sea Lion Caves to watch, far below on the rocks, the playful sport of these noisy sea creatures as they dip and splash in and out of the wave tossed sea. We follow watery steps leading into a cave, the sea lions' chilly winter home. We stand on the damp stone floor and watch the waves explode, pound, echo against the walls. Climbing back into the sunlight, we stand at the top of the cliff and bid farewell to the sea lions on the rock shelf by the ocean. Across the cove is the picturesque Hecata Lighthouse sitting high on a cliff behind a trio of massive sea-stacks.

Later when we stop for a sumptuous seafood lunch in the tiny coastal town of Yachats, our waitress asks if we have taken the ride up to Perpetua Overlook. When given a negative answer, she insists we must turn around and make that trip. We backtrack several miles and bear off the main highway onto the steep, curving road to the heights of the Overlook. What a Gift to have been guided here!

> Perpetua Overlook, highest point of the land,
> forces our earth-bound vision to widely expand.
> The magnificent seascape stretches miles before us;
> we absorb with the eyes of an eagle that soars.

I feel a reverential silence fall upon my spirit. My heart recalls the words of Yahweh's covenant with Noah after the flood: "I now establish my covenant with you and with your descendants after you and with every living creature that was with you ~ the birds, the livestock, and all the wild animals…every living creature on earth" (Genesis 9:9-11). In this setting, these words take on new meaning.

> God made a covenant, not only with humankind,
> but with all living creatures of sea, land, and sky:
> beauty adorns the earth for all to enjoy
> and no favorites will be accorded when gifts are deployed.

> Awed by the awareness of what we all share
> on this rich planet given by Spirit's loving care,
> we bow before the evidence of Creator's faithfulness.
> Through Covenant promises, all creation is blessed.

With fresh awareness, I contemplate the beauty that we are witnessing and my relationship to all of creation. May I be helped to see *all* as divine Gift so my heart may grow in compassion and care-full-ness.

Journal, May 6th-10th

A New Way to Ride–Listening and Following

Leaving Perpetua Overlook, we remain in contemplative silence. In this reflective mood, we ride north to Newport, Oregon, where we need to lay over for a couple of days to rest, relax, and meditate upon the powerful images of the last few days.

When we find that our motel is located within walking distance of the Oregon Coast Aquarium, we decide a visit to this interesting facility fits well into our relaxation plans. Our tour of the Aquarium gifts us with far more than relaxation. The artistry of the architectural design and the playfulness of the sea otters shower us with delight. We wander through the indoor displays of baby sea animals. The infant crabs, newly born skates (one still in its egg case), miniature sea nettles, and fragile baby coral plume anemones, minute replicas of their graceful parents, fascinate us. The Creator's tender attention and care for all life is evidenced here. Our spirits are humbled as we remember that the Covenant promise to "all living creatures" extends even to these tiny, tiny beings.

The greatest joy of the day, however, comes from observing the giant octopus ~ giant here indicating a size of five feet! As we watch, she curls in her cave, moves her arms in gentle gliding motions, and tries to find a comfortable way to settle for sleep. We learn that octopi are one of the few invertebrates that actually sleep. The fearful stories we hear of this species are hard to believe as we gaze at the delicate, gliding movements of this lovely creature.

> She floats in gentle patience,
> her lovely rose body turned away.
> Long sinewy arms glide,
>   curl,
>   tuck,
>   disappear.
>
> Shy, she wishes not our gaze,
> orchestrates her sensuous body
> into her home cave

away from peering eyes
and unwelcome stares.
We who gaze are mesmerized!

Embarrassed for invading the privacy
of this eight tentacled lovely
whose home God made the depths of the sea,
we turn away
and leave this Beauty in Rose

in Water

in Peace.

Deeply touched by the connection we feel to this water creature, we quietly leave the aquarium and return to our motel. The calm of this aquatic sojourn is, unfortunately, short-lived. We allow ourselves to be drawn into wrestling with the question of whether we have enough time to visit all the places on our desired agenda without encountering extremely hot weather when we ride across the high plains. Then we remind ourselves of our commitment to *trust* we will be given the guidance to know if something must be stricken from our agenda!

Feeling very relaxed and rested from our two-day sojourn in Newport, we begin the last day of our ride along the spectacular Oregon coast. Eventually the road turns from the sea to carry us through tranquil pastoral scenery and then curves again to the shore at Cannon Beach. We stop to view Haystack Rock, one of the world's largest monoliths. Standing only a short distance from shore, it majestically guards the beach. This place, however, does not provide a quiet reflective setting. Hundreds of people sprawl across the gleaming sand while dozens of others surf the waves that roll mightily into the cove.

Riding on, we joy in the quiet beauty of the coastal road. By day's end we are nearing Astoria, Oregon. Before entering the city, we take a side trip to visit Fort Clatsop, which is nestled on the shore of the Columbia River. The Fort was built as the winter quarters of Lewis and Clark while they prepared for their return journey east. It was at this location Lewis and Clark's incredibly successful exploration of the Louisiana Purchase reached its end. The celebration over their success must have been shadowed by their failure to find the desired water route to the "Great Western Sea" because the record of their sojourn at Fort Clatsop alludes to "the physical celebration of a journey ended, ...also a sense of incompletion." Standing in this place where such a momentous journey reached its climax and tapping into the feelings of these heroic figures, I am carried into the historic past as an emotionally moving present experience.

Leaving this evocative place, we ride into Astoria. There we settle for the night in a motel room overlooking the expansive Columbia River and the massive suspension bridge that joins the shores of Oregon with those of Washington. Before resuming our journey, we follow our usual custom on Sunday mornings when we are traveling.

> Worshiping in the morning of early First Day,
> We look over the Columbia River.
> Fog rolls in on the mountains beyond
> and settles our hearts with a feeling of calm.
>
> Our day begins in quietness and peace:
> God's gifts to us seem never to cease.
>
> In harbor before us stands a tall post;
> barnacles, moss, and grass it hosts.
> Perched there, the early bird heralds the day
> with chirping songs and flapping wings.

Ready to begin a new adventure, we visit one of the local tourist attractions:

> The Astoria Column, our agenda's first goal.
> Why? Because we should, we are told!
>> 166 steps to the top we must climb!
>> After a few, Fred says, "This adventure's not mine!"
> By a little lady behind us, we are pushed a step at a time ~
> the view from the top is absolutely sublime!

A mural depicting the history of Oregon winds itself to the top of this impressive one hundred and twenty-five foot column. From the top, we have a panoramic view of the Columbia River and the surrounding valley.

Descending the steps, we prepare for our next adventure, a breathtaking ride across the towering Astoria-Megler Bridge into Washington. Then begins a two-day interlude in our journey, during which nothing seems to go "right." Experiencing one mishap after another, we finally give in to the humor of the situation and have a wonderful time laughing along the way:

I. Morning

> Today is a day that is full of merriment;
> everything seems with a sense of fun lent:
>> tiny touch of sunshine, which begins the day,
>> is only a tease soon by clouds pushed away.
> Committing to enjoy whatever the change,
> smiles for clouds seems a good exchange.

> Looking for lunch, we stop to eat.
> Sunday Brunch advertised, seems like a treat:
>> lunch with champagne, which we do not drink,
>> cloth napkins, candles, crystal! All in the pink!
> The gourmet menu seems not to our taste;
> so we leave quietly, in courteous haste.

> We walk the street and seek another place.
> The "Loose Caboose" offers a cozy space.
>> Here the food seems more to our liking,

fish and chips, oysters, and friendliness striking.
A train clock whistles, its locomotive steams;
the forest fruit pie a' la mode is truly a dream!

II. Afternoon

Continuing our ride, we think to the coast;
we never see a wave, despite Washingtonian's boast.
    The closest we come are mud flats in coves,
        sculpted by the waters in various modes.
The rest of the time we ride through the trees;
lovely to see, but far from ocean breeze.

Later, we stop and look at the map.
Why we had missed the coast, we understand in a snap.
    For the main road goes through hill, cove and trees,
        while the scenic route curves along the coast and sea.
Why did we not take the scenic route then?
We know not! It is just how, so far, this day has been.

The time for afternoon coffee begins a new search;
surely there will be Espresso along this stretch.
    Two or three scattered houses comprise a town,
        but a cup of coffee is nowhere to be found.
Finally we arrive at Boondockers Coffee Café;
for only coffee, however, we seem in the way.

III. Evening

When we arrive in Aberdeen, where we
will stay for the night,
    timber industry strikers wave and smile at our sight.
This town is a throwback to the place of my childhood where
    buildings' empty shells, among modern structures, stood.
Riverfront ruins are the view from our room.
Not to mind! Our motorcycle makes the hotel workers swoon.

And what do we make of the mirth of this day?
For our spiritual journeys does it have a message to say?
    Perhaps that God has a fun side, likes a good laugh,
    and helps us find joy on unexpected paths.
As we come to the end of this funny day,
we smile as heads upon pillows we lay.

The ability to laugh at our predicament is a saving factor in the morning when we wake to realize we are stranded for another day, in Aberdeen, Washington, far from the coast.

The rain pours down as we awake to new day.
It seems the trip to the coast will have another delay.
    Can we continue to laugh and the mirth in this see,
    as we search for the lesson that must here be.
So in comfort at least, we settle down,
to wait out the rain in this ancient river town.

We wonder and ponder how we could have pulled such a blooper,
when views on the coast are supposed to be super.
    With map not at hand, we blundered along.
    Message: "Without God's roadmap, lives can go wrong!"
We determine to laugh at our human mistakes,
and rejoice in the rain for the good of souls' sake.

Today is the first time since we left Florida that we have had to lay over somewhere because of rain. Seeing our situation in this larger perspective, we relax and look forward to a quiet day.

As I review our journey so far, especially the experiences of the last ten days, I am led to reflect on my "call" to be a *traveling contemplative*. This call must be lived into if it is to become a reality. I do not choose the time, the place, or the medium in which the divine Presence is experienced or through which Spirit's messages are given. All the variety of life is the time, place, and medium through which Mystery slips into my awareness and then vanishes. My control over this experience is totally lacking. The only task I can perform is to be awake to the moment and open to receive. The rest is all Gift!

After a wonderful day of reading, reflection, and rest, we retire for the night at peace with whatever the morrow will bring. Morning brings a song of praise:

> Rejoice, oh heart!
> The morn has come,
> rain has passed,
> blue sky is born.
> Broken clouds float,
> puffy and white.
> Temperature is cool,
> breeze is still.
>
> A prayer of petition
> prepares our way:
> "May Spirit lead
> to the glorious sea."

Leaving Aberdeen to ride north, we soon see the sun fade and we encounter a gentle misty rain. This dampness is not totally unexpected because we are entering the rainforest area of Washington. Here on the Olympic coast, we will have to wear rain suits for the first time in the almost 7000 miles we have traveled.

Our spirits match the rains as we view the extensive clear-cutting of the old growth forests. Here in Washington, as in Oregon, we look out on acres of stumps, broken limbs and twigs. Off in the distance we view striped hills; they appear that way because of the pattern of clear-cutting where one third of the forest growth is retained while two-thirds of the hill is stripped of all trees. Along the road, the new growth woodlands have signs posted periodically to tell the date when these lands were clear-cut or commercially thinned. The sadness we feel is eased somewhat by new trees being planted to replace what has been cut. There is, however, an enormous contrast between true forest and a stand of commercially planted trees, which are all the same age, all the same size, all lined in neat rows. The variety of forest plants inhabiting natural forests are not provided entry in these manicured woodlands.

This evident contrast reawakens our sadness and sense of loss as we ride into the shelter of the protected rainforest. Hiking under these venerable trees dripping with ferns and moss, we feel their spirits touch our spirits and a song rises from my heart:

> God gives a model for true community
> in the old growth forest's canopy.
> Competition is not the by-word here;
> cooperation is necessary to all, it is clear.
>
> A complete ecosystem is birthed in these forests:
> over thousands of years building what is before us.
> Each part has its own contribution to make,
> For the health of this fragile system is at stake.
>
> The lowliest lichen, mosses, fungi, and bacteria
> are as important as stately fir, hemlock, and spruce called Sitka,
> for they hold in the canopy moisture of rain and fog,
> and work to decompose and provide nutrients
> from decaying old logs.
>
> In true forest the trees come in all ages, sizes, and shapes;
> holes in overripe trees, homes and food for birds, insects, and
> small mammals make.
> The grandfather trees that have fallen never die,
> but are recycled into burrows, nutrients, and tiny new trees
> growing from their sides.
>
> Glacial rivers slide out and cut through the land
> carrying rock slivers, desiccated creatures,
> and forest detritus to the strand.
> Swept into the sea and caught by currents
> they cross the wide ocean
> to provide nutrients needed for fish population.
>
> Natural disasters wipe out some places, small pieces,
> for a short time,
> but leave essential stronger elements alive or dormant for awhile.
> Human destruction ~ clear-cutting and pollution ~

> destroys everything in large sections; no hope for renewal of
> forest's condition.
>
> Dying and decay are part of life's cycle;
> life may spring forth in new intricacies.
> Whether it is a forest or a human community,
> the rules are the same: All of life is a unity.
> Humankind must respect nature's rhythm,
> and work in concert with the Divine life pattern.

Surrounded by a wild and extravagant variety of plant life, we follow a path into the rainforest that leads to the Magnificent Largest Sitka Spruce in the World: 191 feet tall, 58 feet in circumference, 96 foot root span, and approximately 1000 years old. We stand, honoring its presence, as the rain drips down our faces. As we leave the sacred stillness of this place, our bodies receive through touch the message spoken by Spirit of nature's rhythm. The path beneath our feet is softened by the remnants of what was once vibrant life. Leaves, cones, needles, insects, and branches now lie lifeless on the forest floor and the path is edged in places by the decaying logs of fallen trees. Yet, from this lifeless debris, new life springs forth ~ tiny plants dot the path as we walk gently and seek not to crush this budding newness. Small trees, replicas of their fallen ancestors, now lift their infant greenery from the decaying forms beneath them that will nourish what is being born. This divine pattern of new life from death makes very real the Truth of the message: Unless a seed falls to the ground and dies, it cannot produce new life (John 12:24).

When we return to our bike, our spirits are alive with a new appreciation for the wisdom embedded in nature by Creator God. Riding from the shelter of the rainforest, we stop for a moment to share gazes with a shy Roosevelt elk. To have seen this lovely creature in the wild, even for a moment, is a graced touch bringing to a close our rainforest interlude.

Journal, May 10th-16th

Turning Point

10

The road turns north and hugs the coast as we leave the rainforest. Our longing hearts rejoice at the sound and sight of the sea. Our destination today is the picturesque Kalaloch Lodge where we fulfill one of the dreams we have for this trip: to rent a cabin for a few days either along the coast or in the mountains. At Kalaloch, our cabin is situated on a bluff overlooking the Pacific Ocean far below. We are barely settled into our cozy habitat when the misty drizzle, in which we have ridden all day, turns into a heavy downpour. It matters little! We sit in our breakfast nook and have lunch while we watch the ocean through the rain-draped windowpanes. What a perfect place this is to spend our last days along the coast. I joy in this Gift and watch

> Nature writes her own sweet poetry,
> Hymns of praise to Creator who formed Her:
> > white waves cresting the incoming tide
> > small creek out-flowing enveloped by sea
> > tree limbs rustling an evening wind song
> > plants and insects buzzing celebration
> > brown birds pecking for tiny dinner bugs
> > white and yellow daisies glowing festively
> > buttercups and grasses dancing the breeze.
>
> Nature's very Being, a wonder of beauty untold.
> In listening to Her poetry, we find food for our souls.

A New Way to Ride–Listening and Following

Our little cabin at Kalaloch Lodge shelters us for two nights. The rain abates on the second day and we have an opportunity to walk down to the beach. The piles of driftwood make evident the reason for cautious warnings visitors are given to beware of walking along the shore in a storm. Threatening harm to anyone on the beach, huge logs are often thrown on shore by the storm-tossed waves. On this quiet sunny day, however, we walk beside a calm sea and among the piles of driftwood. The artistic shapes of some of these pieces and the beautiful grains in the wood fascinate us. The open beach, upon which they lie, curves along the edges of a rapidly flowing stream. In stark contrast to the image of a powerful stormy sea, this stream forms quiet pools mirroring trees on shore and driftwood logs resting within the tranquil waters.

As the day comes to a close, we stand on the bluff and watch the sunset paint the sky in glorious colors and splash shimmering rose across the crests of the waves. These quiet moments at Kalaloch Lodge help prepare our spirits for the rapidly approaching day when we must say our farewell to the sea.

On our last morning here, I watch, through rain-streaked windows, the blurred image of a robin in front of our cabin as I recall the moments of these lovely days.

Sitting at my window in our ocean-side hermitage,
I savor the blessings given me here by the sea:
robin sitting on fence post
chirping the dawn;
raccoon scurrying under deck
away from the storm;
primitive beach filled
with forest debris ~
huge logs and tree trunks being sculpted
and weathered by the sea;
great ocean waves rolling in
under gray skies and sun;

Turning Point

   river's swift current plummeting
     down to the surf;
   clouds gray and pink covering
     evening sky;
   sun setting radiantly
   on bluffs high above shore;
   birds dancing an evening song
   over cove and through trees;
   fresh salmon dinners prepared
     deliciously;
   graceful evergreens towering
     against blue sky;
   quiet, calling my spirit away
     from all cares.

With thankfulness and joy, my heart abounds;
To say good-bye to the coast, my spirit is now free.

  In a very light misty rain, we leave this place of quiet repose. Not being familiar with the character of rainforests, we unintentionally have not given adequate respect to the weather. We assume that rain gear will not be needed in this gentle mist. How wrong we are! The rain never becomes heavy, but as the road edges the coast for a short distance and then turns inland along the Hoh River, the constant heavy mist, combined with temperatures in the forties, makes for a cold, damp, miserable ride. There is no place to stop and put on our rain suits. By the time we reach Forks, forty miles to the north, we are thoroughly wet and cold. Our plan was to ride out to La Push on the coast where some of the most amazing sea-stacks rise from the ocean. The experience of the morning, however, makes us leery of jumping into such an adventure. We visit the Ranger Station where we are warned to expect this misty rain on the entire fifty-mile ride to the coast and back. It sounds as though another Divine "detour" is guiding us away from this trip.

An alternative enjoyment is offered at a local restaurant ~ a delicious, warming bowl of soup with salad and coffee. Feeling somewhat refreshed, we heed the lesson of the morning's ride and don our rain gear. On the trip to Port Angeles, the warmth provided by our rain suits ensures a more pleasant ride. Our spirits lift as the road twists through serene countryside. We are sheltered on one side of the road by the caressing shadow of the rainforest and on the other side we gaze at an alpine setting surrounding the pristine glacier-carved, Crescent Lake.

At the head of the lake, the road winds down the mountain to Port Angeles. This major port nestles along the edge of the Strait of Juan de Fuca, which separates Washington from Vancouver Island, Canada. The city is built on a hill overlooking the Strait. The expanse of picture windows in our motel suite looks over both the Strait and the snow-covered Olympic Range. Once again, we have been led to a quiet, tranquil setting that is ideal for reflecting on our journey.

> To be aware of what is given
> is to live in Grace.
> Every day with gold is leavened,
> Spirit's treasure
> beyond measure,
> if in our hearts we allow God space.

Our morning ride has dampened our hope to make one special trip before leaving the Pacific Coast for good. During our stay in Port Angeles, we want to ride to the westernmost tip of Washington ~ Cape Flattery. The constant rain of the last few days, however, makes us wonder if this will be a possibility. If we are to make this trip, we trust "way will open."

In the early morning, the clouds are painted with peach light from the rising sun. The snow and glacier capped mountains of the Olympic Range glisten under the light of a thin crescent moon. The Strait is still; no breeze ruffles the waters. Across the

Strait rise the mountains of Vancouver Island. As we watch the dawn unfold, we wonder what the day will bring.

> The morning breaks glorious
> with sunshine and warmth!
>
> Today we will ride
> to Cape Flattery,
> the end of the land
> where horizon meets sea!

We excitedly ready ourselves for the seventy-mile trip along the Strait of Juan de Fuca. The road twists and turns through small towns, mountain passes, and finally along the stunning scenery of the coast. The day is chilly and our ride is only slightly warmed by the sunshine, but the joy of our spirits overcomes the chill. When the road enters Neah Bay, a small town on the Makah Indian Reservation and the last settlement along the coast, we know we are nearing our destination. Filled with anticipation, we ride through town toward the road that will take us to the Cape. Then, suddenly, we are confronted with an unexpected development that resonates with fears from the past:

> After leaving the paved road at Neah Bay,
> we turn onto a dirt/gravel pathway.
> To ride on gravel roads we have vowed never to do;
> Spirit commands, "Go forward! Do not be afraid!"

The four-mile journey on this gravel road, during which we try to swallow our uneasiness, culminates at the beginning of a path arbored by trees.

> A wooden plank walkway leads through rainforest.
> The moist stillness secrets breathtaking beauty:
>   turquoise sea splashes against mountainous cliffs,
>   rolls into huge caves carved by pounding waves.

> Someday these bluffs will fall into the sea
> as ocean cuts away rock over centuries.
>
> This sacred place where the eternal sea
> meets the elegant bounty of cove and shore
> forms Creator's haven
> to birds and sea creatures
> and fully nourishes their lives in beauty and joy.
>
> All the beauty I see now only speaks peace!
> I stand on the coast where lands cease;
> the sea stretches before me endlessly.
> I gaze on the ocean that carves the cliffs
> and watch the waves crash thunderously.
> This journey has carved spiritual caves in my heart,
> into which flows Living Water, giving my life a new start.

We understand well why the Native Americans consider Cape Flattery sacred ground. Here the sea bestows its benediction blessing upon our journey as we stand in sacred silence. As our spirits soar out into this endless vista, our hearts, rooted in the earth, know this as the turning point in our journey. There are no more roads to carry us along the sea or westward into the unknown. Now all roads will lead toward home. Awareness of this climactic moment in our journey brings tears of sadness mixed with joy. Our hearts are so full we speak no words as we walk back through the rainforest.

No longer fearful, we slowly make the return trip on the gravel road to Neah Bay. Searching for a place for lunch, we take the recommendation of a local man. The Makah Maiden Café is a Native American owned restaurant, where we enjoy fresh halibut, salad, mashed potatoes, fresh baked bread, and blackberry pie. Bodies, as well as spirits, now refreshed, we begin the journey back to Port Angeles. Along the way, we stop to walk the beach along the Strait. Off shore stands a gigantic sea-stack from the top of which a tree reaches for the sky. Soft waves lick the shore of

Turning Point

the beach, littered with nature's gifts: huge logs, tree stumps, varied colored rocks, seaweed strands, and crab shells. Reluctantly we leave this westward shore and resume our ride.

In the evening, I meditate on the meaning of today's trip for my own spiritual path.

> We are at the turning point in our journey,
>   physically land's end, today at Cape Flattery.
> What does this mean for journey of spirit?
>   I can only listen for the answer, pray to hear it.
>   I feel so at peace, in tune with all creation.
> Only one word describes ~ Elation!

As I continue to journal of my day's experience, I suddenly feel as though the gift of poetry is being withdrawn. There is flatness, an emptiness that permeates what I want to express on the page. I wonder if this seeming absence of Divine Spirit after such a powerful awareness of God's presence is another step along the spiritual path. As I seek to stay in this moment, live into this feeling, ironically, the very question I am raising finds expression in verse:

> Strange I find the place I'm in,
>   as our journey reaches land's end.
> The poetry that was given
>   to speak my heart
>   no longer sings within my soul.
> What is the message I'm being told?

> Through windows I gaze upon mountain peaks,
>   glorious, in snow and glacier steeped.
> Is my voice to be frozen deep within
>   just at the time
>   when my heart breaks free?
> With peace endowed, my head is bowed.

> Sunset gleams rose on the mountain snow
> and in my heart there is one thing I know:
> > whether poetry flows or becomes a dry well,
> > > God is present with me and "All will be well!"
> Aware of Divine Presence in all that I see,
> I am shown how to grow into what I should be.

At peace, I retire for the night to wake early for my usual pre-dawn cup of coffee with God. One lone star shines brightly. The glacier capped mountains of the Olympic Range stand silhouetted against the morning sky ~ no fog and clouds subdue their majestic presence. The sky over the Strait of Juan de Fuca glows pink in the early morning. The waters of the Strait churned into a tossing sea of white caps last night, now lie still and mirror the rose tinted sky. I open the window to hear the dawn! There is only quiet! Even the birds seem hesitant to break the stillness ~ floating, not flying. The wind, which yesterday whipped trees, bushes, flowers, and people into whirling dances of chill beauty, is now still. Only a gentle breeze moves the most fragile branches in a graceful flow of morning praise. The scenes and sounds of this Sunday morning lie like a prayer upon my spirit.

> Peace settles on my life like a morning breeze;
> My heart at last is now at ease.
> The white capped turmoil of the Strait
> Was my heart's own until this date.
> Love has stepped in,
> Its presence real.

> The sun rises brilliant on this morn;
> Spreads Divine glow upon my life.
> In this quiet dawning, I receive
> Beauty which settles my heart
> As the wonder of the coast
> I now must leave.

Turning Point

Grateful for blessings, which Creation shares,
I ride in peace and trust in God's care.

Awareness of the Eternal covenanted presence in all of creation has graced our travels. Our only requirement is to be open, to listen, and to follow Spirit's guidance. As we reach this turning point in our journey and face our Wing toward home, still over 4000 miles away, we go forth from this place calm and in a spirit of peace.

Journal, May 15th-20th

Memories of the beauty of the Pacific flow like waves over our spirits as we ride east. From Port Angeles along the Strait of Juan de Fuca to Port Townsend, the

lovely quiet roads
shadowed by towering trees,
quiet lakes and tranquil coves,
bathe souls in peace.

From Port Townsend, a ferry ride across the rolling bay carries us to the jagged peninsula of the mainland where we ride north to the city of Mount Vernon, Washington. This first night on our journey toward home is filled with memories of the powerful experiences, both physical and spiritual, through which we have been *led* thus far. Our thoughts then drift to the question: "What will be given in the rest of our journey?"

The remembering and anticipation, however, do not inhibit our ability to sleep. We wake rested and ready to see what this day will bring. The morning portion of our trip is through pastoral Skagit Valley.

In soft green pastures horses and cattle graze
near mirror ponds reflecting back their gaze.
Snow covered mountains
rise heavenward in the distance.

Detouring into Rockport State Park, we stop under old growth trees:

> The lush dripping shade
> of rainforest stillness
> descends on our spirits
> with ethereal hush.
>
> Our quiet picnic
> now is joined
> by a friendly woman,
> a Gold Wing fan.
> Her distant memories
> we evoke
> and stir her longing
> to ride far from home.

Alone once again, we sit under these trees among the ferns, moss, fungi, decaying logs, and sprouting new trees and we feel "at home." These companions of creation summon from deep within the joy of fleeting moments spent in the rainforest along the coast. It is almost as through the Divine Spirit is gentling us into our new landscape by offering a moment to bask in memory.

Now it is time to move on. We ride through the valley toward snow-covered mountains.

> Glacier fed streams coursing through the land
> leave islands of rock, gravel, and sand.
> Puffy wool llamas in coats of white, brown, and tan
> roam luscious green pastures aesthetically planned.

When we reach the mountains of Cascades National Park, the road climbs to higher altitudes where strangely it is very warm even where snow is still packed along edges of the road.

> Soaring Douglas firs reach upward toward sky,
> Splashing waterfalls slide down the mountain,

Sheer rock cliffs rise beside the road,
And eagles float on wind currents toward Spirit's abode.

Glacier-tipped mountains touch pristine blue sky,
A frozen white mantle that glistens Divine glory.
Rocky bluffs hang menacingly over our heads,
but in God's presence there is no dread.

The quiet glory of these granite mountains bursts forth in a visual musical concert:

Snow lies on mountain's cleft like a musical score:
great granite spires *crescendo* toward heaven,
river of snow flows in *adagio*,
waterfalls bounce on rocks in sparkling *staccato*.

Fragile leaves of aspen flutter like musical wind chimes,
dance in the breeze as in ancient times.
Birds, like flute notes, trill high and low.
This musical *concerto*, Creator's love does bestow.

Our hearts filled with the mountain's music, we end our day's journey when we happen upon the rustic elegance of a mountain lodge surrounded by forests and fronted by a tranquil lake. Here at Freestone Inn in Mazama, Washington, we enjoy a delicious dinner after which a deeply nurturing Sabbath silence descends.

Ducks float on the movement of lake's current,
never asking if the way is right or is errant.
They are content to be carried wherever the lake pleases,
gradually brought to safe haven on the lake's grassy edges.

Amazing how gently life moves in quiet places:
To nature's voice it listens,
Graces all of creation.

Sitting in log-hewn chairs on the porch of our room, we watch the silent dawn slowly dispel the night darkness. A beautiful foretaste of the coming phase of our journey!

Coffee by the lake in the early predawn
as sky lightens from black to luminous blue
of morn.
Stars many and brilliant in the dark night sky,
now fading and fewer as light begins to arise.

Cradled in this valley among mighty mountains,
this quiet refuge provides spirit with water
from Divine fountain.
The lake, a looking-glass reflection of the beauty that surrounds,
as the Infinite is imaged in each soul's ground.

Sound of human machines in the distance is heard;
breeze ripples the lake and nature's image
is blurred.
Times of peaceful retreat needed, the Divine image to see,
if we are to become the persons we are intended to be.

Patiently waiting nature's surprise,
over the mountain, we watch Morning Star
in its brilliant rise.
Shining upon us ~ God's beloved children ~ we see
True Life calling us in gentle plea.

The clouds now are painted in muted tones of rose.
Gradually the landscape emerges from night's
blanketed abode:
trees, animals, and mountains come clearly into view.
The quiet is held in hearts made new.

The morning begins with creature's songs of praise:
fish break lake's surface, joy ripples
out in rays;

geese give thanks as morning manna they gather;
birds dip and float in choreographed pattern.

The hush permeating this place
gives a taste of the harmony with which
Creator's world is graced.
Allowing the stillness to settle life's hectic pace,
we become merged into the wonder of eternity's space.

Feeling enormously blessed by the scenes of beauty through which we have journeyed and the peace of this tranquil place among the mountains, we ready ourselves to follow the path given for this day. We are learning to joy in the gift of one day at a time as we leave the future to the Spirit Wind.

Journal, May 20th-22nd

Spirit's Roadmap Brings Joy

11

We find it difficult to leave the tranquil setting of the Freestone Inn and the eloquent beauty of Cascades National Park:

> Surrounded by mountains in valleys of quiet,
> riding near glaciers, on mountain tops silent,
> we want to stay!
> God's presence is so tangible:
> "Let us hold on to these moments," we pray.

It is not given us to hold on. The road draws us forward on a new path, to new adventures. During our ride toward Spokane, Washington, the world is alive with Divine messages:

> How like life is the landscape today:
> such a variety of scenes, creatures, and delights.
> The total of these tell the story of life,
> as we journey through periods of joy or strife.
>
> A cemetery on a hill with crosses of gold,
> horses in a field nursing their foals,
> transitions of death and birth are part of this road
> and we celebrate both as part of the whole.

In the miles and miles of unspectacular forest, the trees change in almost imperceptible stages from spruce to fir to Ponderosa pine. This evolution speaks to our spirits of the slow progression of ordinary days when life offers no special joys or

A New Way to Ride–Listening and Following

sorrows, and growth seems to languish. Lulled into daydreaming by this scenery, we are suddenly shaken from our musing when we round a curve and emerge from the forest. Unexpected vistas of high desert call forth a visceral longing for the barrenness and solitude that invited such wondrous periods of inner growth and healing. Further along the road, the desert yields to rocky hills. The constantly changing images of the landscape resonate with our spiritual journeys and the events of our lives.

> Great boulders loom over our heads,
> send huge rocks tumbling down to road bed.
> Shattering events roll into our lives
> and carry away plans in an avalanche of surprise.

From this sobering scene, we enter an area of deep canyons imaging the caverns of despair into which we can be drawn, but then the landscape offers a vision of hope:

> Swift flowing river courses from canyon to flood plain;
> horses, cattle, sheep graze in luscious green pastures.
> Vast cultivated fields image the wonder times
> when Living Water pours into our hearts and heals pain,
> and our lives yield the fruits of the Spirit.

The massive Grand Coulee Dam suddenly dominates the scene and evokes mixed feelings. We rejoice that it provides water for cultivation and power to homes. At the same time, its dominance over the entire vista is a graphic reminder that humankind's efforts to control creation for our own purposes must be done in concert with the Divine plan if these efforts are to benefit *all* life.

Immersed as we are in contemplative awareness of the scenes around us, we are surprised to feel summer heat descending as we ride. The severe discomfort we feel forces us to acknowledge that our bodies no longer adjust well to such scorching temperatures. Dealing with such heat is a major consideration because we have several thousand summer-miles yet to ride before reaching home.

Spirit's Roadmap Brings Joy

Our concern is visualized in the landscape as our gaze rests wearily on

> railroad tracks in a path
> across the hot open land
> into the steaming horizon,
> calling us home.

Wilted by the heat, we arrive in Spokane, Washington, for a few days rest and time to seek guidance for the remainder of our trip. Our desire is to see some of Idaho and Montana, slip into Utah to visit our son, then travel on through Wyoming, South Dakota, and finally up into the high plains of North Dakota. No leading is forthcoming from our Spirit Guide at this juncture. It is bewildering, but we also are aware that we must be patient, listen, and be ready to hear when the Voice finally speaks.

From Spokane, we ride through the scenic northern portion of Idaho into the Cabinet Mountains Wilderness of Montana. We are not fully entering the experience, however, because our minds are entangled with uncertainty over what our path should be. Traveling along Route 2, through the Rocky Mountains, my head is filled with concerns, daydreams, and worries. I am not present to what is before us. As we round a curve in the road, suddenly and powerfully,

> The Mountain rises before my face,
> Sheer wall granite ~
> Strong, massive, yet protective ~
> Full of Spirit.
> It bows my heart
> And then my face
> Before its presence,
> Not in fear but holy awe.
> Moses-like,
> I want to fall face down,
> Acknowledge this as holy ground,

> God's dwelling place.
> In shelter of these granite tabernacles,
> I am held for eternity's moment
> In Divine embrace.
> Oh such Grace!
> My heart does sing its silent praise;
> With joy it rings ~
> For I see the face of God
> In this stone and glacial mountain,
> And I live!
> That Image planted within recognizes Itself ~
> New Life begins.

We ride on in sacred silence! The massive Rocky Mountains hold us in Divine tenderness until we arrive in West Glacier, Montana where we settle into a timeworn, but comfortable, motel with a stunning view of the mountains. We unpack our bike and ride off to enjoy time in Glacier National Park. Our dream of riding the spectacular Going-To-The-Sun-Road is shattered when we are told that, because of snow, only sixteen miles of the Park road are open. It appears that Divine Guidance is issuing a wake-up call for us to re-examine our travel plans. The message is disappointingly clear: Another of God's "detours!"

> The weather has served as the instrument
> to mark Divine "detours" all along our way.
> We chose the mountains. Spirit said, "No!"
> We sought the coast without delay
> "No! The desert is where you must stay!"

> Our present plan is through mountains to roam
> and finally end at our son's Utah home.
> Summer is suddenly in the air;
> in Utah heat, we will not fare well.
> The Going-To-The-Sun-Road that we wish to ride
> is hidden by avalanche under eighty feet of snow.

News arrives from home of a dear friend's distress.
God, you are sure making of our plans a mess!

Learning to follow our hearts, not our heads,
to listen and go wherever we are led,
to welcome with joy Divine plan for each day,
is not as easy to do, as it is to say.

Our feelings of disappointment evaporate during the sublime rides that we make on the sixteen miles of road that are open. The turbulent rivers of the Park refresh our spirits as we stand on the bridges or overlooks and watch the

    river gushing, roaring along its path,
        tumbling,
            foaming,
                cascading;
full with spring life!
Fed by glacial melt from mountain top,
    clearing,
        cleansing
living water refreshes the land
with joy.

Being open to God's presence in all things
Brings us joy and makes our hearts sing.

Our hearts echo the bubbling, tossing, dancing, falling rivers and our bodies rejoice as we feast on delicious mountain trout taken from such streams. The sparkling pristine lakes mirror the towering, snow-crowned mountains. We walk the shores of these lakes and sit on large boulders just off shore. A sense of peace enfolds us. Our wills bend in grateful acceptance of the "detour" that has been directed.

We now must turn our faces and our hearts toward home. Our plans for extensive travel in this section of the nation await another journey. On our last morning here in Glacier National

Park, we view the snow-capped peaks of the Rockies emerging from the pre-dawn mist. The image is a powerful metaphor of the Transcendent:

> Divine Mystery reveals itself
> if I have eyes to see or ears to hear.
>
> Mountain peaks
> from night's cover emerge
> against glow of morning sky.
> Trees
> unveiled from palette of darkness,
> unique shapes
> sketched against divine mist
> of mountain fog.
> Whispered stillness of early morn:
> no breeze,
> no animal sounds.
> Eternal quiet resting upon the land.
>
> Mighty mountains embrace earth with
>   Presence,
>   Beauty,
>   Power ~
> Holy hills from which flow Living Water.
>
> Divine Mystery, unveil my spirit,
> my beloved uniqueness reveal;
> Spirit's water-fall into my being,
> that spring Life may
>   clear,
>   clean,
>   refresh,
>   and fill.

Serenely, we greet the dawn and say farewell to these granite mountains of immanent Presence.

Journal, May 22nd-27th

Leaving our vintage motel, we follow the curving road along the southern edge of the Park and then north toward East Glacier. The eastern mountain landscape evidences clearly that snow and rain are mostly captured on the western slopes. Patches of snow on these eastern peaks are in stark contrast to the burnished brown and tan stone of the lower slopes.

The tranquility of our ride turns to disquiet as we experience our first exposure to the high plains. This feeling of trepidation is soon dispelled, however, as we are touched by the solitude and vast openness of this land. The boundlessness embraces our spirits and we feel held in the eternal immensity of the universe. The scene grips us with an awe-filled intensity of Presence. A momentary glimpse of the Eternal! The wind carries Spirit's whisper:

> "No more mountains to climb, My child;
> Bask in the rolling hills of My Love for awhile.
> Lay yourself open, like the great stretching plains,
> And let Spirit blow over.
> Life ~ tranquil and sane."

My spirit opens and floats a whispered response upon the winds:

> These vast open spaces touch our souls,
> Enfold our spirits in Sacred Mystery.
> We are but specks in this spacious landscape,
> Yet, we are formed in the Divine image.
>
> We wonder what it feels like to live in this place,
> To experience one's self constantly in eternity's space.
> There is no hiding from self, or God, here.
> All is so open we feel the immensity
> Of God's loving covenant.

All day we ride, held in the infinite solitude, stillness, openness, and serenity of these plains that stretch out in grassy carpet for miles until they vanish into the horizon or the far, far distant mountains. I feel as if my spirit could simply merge into this universe. Our connection with the plains remains intact during our overnight stay in the small town of Havre, Montana. As I spend time with my journal, I offer a prayer of thankfulness for being led into this hallowed land and for the gift of poetry that has been given; no medium, other than verse, could truly express the powerful experience of this day.

Leaving Havre, we guide the Wing back onto Route 2. Known as the "Hi-Line," this highway cuts a direct path across the northernmost quarter of Montana and North Dakota. As we travel this lonely open road,

> the wind whistles across the high plains;
> the spirits of those who wandered here moan their pain.
> We are carried into the heart of the Great Spirit,
> by feelings of compassion for those whose blood soaked this sod.

The Nez Perce were one group of Native Americans whose blood this soil tasted. Joseph, their chief, has long been one of my heroes.

> Trying to reach freedom and escape persecution,
> a noble chief, for many miles through this land, led his people.
> To relieve their suffering, he made a noble gesture:
> "I will fight no more forever!" To that promise he held true.

We turn from the main highway and ride many miles deep into the plains. I want to stand at the place where Chief Joseph surrendered after an agonizing trek of hundreds of miles to escape the pursuing United States army. The tribe stopped to rest, here at Bear Paw Battlefield, only a day's journey from the freedom of Canada. The army caught up with them. The winds carry woeful voices, which cut deep into the spirit.

We turn away from this place of sad remembrance to make the lengthy journey back to the main road. The picturesque sight of pronghorn antelope grazing on the open expanse of fresh spring grasses eases the sadness of our hearts. Riding further through the tilled fields of these plains, we turn our mind's gaze to the early settlers who toiled over the years to build a new life in these oceans of grass. Their voices at first whisper a joyous tale, one that later cries loss and grief.

>Those pioneers who came to farm this land,
>body and soul plowed into a future plan.
>It all turned to dust and their spirits despaired;
>the land, exhausted, needed time to repair.
>
>It took the death of this land for awareness to grow:
>it is with love and care for the earth we must sow.
>If greed takes over and exploitation wins out,
>the earth will yield until its exhaustion it shouts.

The breeze, here on the high plains, sings many songs and carries many tales.

>The winds now bring a song of joy
>for the lessons learned were willingly employed
>by others who came and with patience repaired the land.
>Hearing the earth, they cooperated with creation's plan.
>Lessons about life was one rich reward
>and a bounty of food from their struggle and toil.
>God has provided for all if we share the yield.

Our vision floats forward in time and we hear modern voices whose song is one of hope and possibility. The tiny town of Saco, Montana, still maintains the tiny white schoolhouse Chet Huntley attended. Huntley was one of my favorite news commentators. Our guidebook says we must call and make an appointment if we wish to visit the schoolhouse. We decide we must forego the pleasure of visiting this site because we are not able to predict with any accuracy when or where we will be. As we are riding along Route 2 in Montana, the road edges the tiny town of Saco. I suddenly spy a small white building beside the road. The only word I can catch as we ride by is "Huntley." I call out to Fred, "Stop! Turn around! I think that is Chet Huntley's schoolhouse." Once again in this journey we are stopped in our tracks, turned around to retrace our path, in order to receive another of Spirit's gifts. Finding the door of the little white building unlocked, we enter and are greeted by a photo display of Huntley's early school years. The classroom remains just as it was when he attended; the traditional pot-bellied stove stands in the center of the room. I am deeply moved and inspired to be standing in this place where the future of a person whom I greatly admire began to be formed:

> Chet Huntley was birthed in a tiny Montana town.
> From a one-room schoolhouse, he became a newsman of renown.
> Lesson: education depends less on size, buildings, or dollars
> than on intellect, desire, and dedication of teachers and scholars.
>
> The harvest of these plains in both food and persons
> Is the inspirited bounty of God's love and generosity.

During our evening in Glasgow, Montana, we share impressions of this enriching day. The enduring gift of these plains appears very clear: it is the heroic spirits who continue to ride these winds and speak messages of courage and fortitude to those who are granted the privilege of experiencing this vast land.

Reflections drift through our dreams and merge into the quiet wonder we feel when we continue our ride across the "Hi-Line." As we near the Montana border, the road dips southward and passes through the lower portion of Fort Peck Indian Reservation and into North Dakota. The landscape offers no clue to having passed from one state into another and, without the "Welcome" sign, our crossing the border would have occurred without notice. For two days, we drift along in the spirit of this quiet, still land and enjoy the images offered as we ride.

> The "Hi-Line" stretches across Montana/Dakota land
> like a ribbon laid upon the vastness it spans. On its journey,

it passes fields, lakes, hills, and occasionally
spills into a town.

This road allows a vista of the expanse of these plains:
for a moment, lets one grasp
what it takes to maintain these flowing fields of grain
that feed our nation.
Our hearts bow in wonder that the earth is so generous.

In the midst of these fields,
rocks are piled in an oval of grass
reminding of the struggle to clear this land
and the joy of overcoming hardship
with Spirit's helping hand.

Wind-breaks
protect fields from howling winds that harm.
Flowering bushes and trees shelter houses
and add beauty to farms.

On ponds and rivulets in the fields and hills,
ducks of all sizes float, tranquil and still.
Mothers with their babies; dads sometimes tag along.
Ripples on the water lend their song.

In what appears as an expanse of wide-open space,
A variety of gifts displays Creator's loving grace.

    To remain in the embrace of these plains with which we feel such unity, we make a three-day stop over in Minot, North Dakota. Nearing the end of this vast openness, we are filled with both gratitude and sadness. Gratitude for the simple joy of having the opportunity to spend seven days in this land of spacious wonder! Gratitude for the "detours" that bring us to these plains in near perfect seventy-degree weather! Sadness at seeing our time here at an end! These plains have drawn my spirit into their expanse. A part of me will ever remain to ride the winds with the spirits of others whose lives have been nourished by this land.

Our Minot retreat time over, we ride back into the powerful winds along the "Hi-Line." While exhilarating, they make trying to hold the bike steady quite a challenge. Fifty miles into this blustery trip, we pause at Rugby, North Dakota, to take pictures in front of the stone tower marking the Geographic Center of North America. The marker becomes a spiritual beacon calling our spirits to the Center, the Source of all the beauty surrounding us. My awareness intensifies and I allow my imagination to carry my spirit into the story and images of this soul-stirring land:

> As a window, I stare from the abandoned farmhouse
> and hear cries, laughter, cheers, which once rang out
> when life within was vibrant and moving,
> now only a memory,
> sweet with longing.
>
> I float with the ducks among the reeds,
> flutter with red-wing blackbird's ease,
> graze with the pronghorn antelope
> and roll in joy
> over the land's gentle slope.
>
> I drift as the clouds while they form a high bank
> moving along, with no goal,
> changing shapes and colors depending on mood ~
> do I want fluffy white joy
> or gray ragged gloom?
>
> Bouncing and floating as winds kick up waves,
> I skim along the surface of Devil's Lake
> surrounded by clouds, trees, and greenery of late.
> While the lake mirrors all,
> with my reflection, I play.

> Spirit moves within all of creation
> bringing wonder and cause for celebration!
> I lift my heart in thanks to God
> for drawing me into this unity with all.

This playful, enlivening last day in the high plains has filled my spirit with joy. I feel like a beloved child who has been blessed with the wonderful surprise gift a Loving Parent has held back until a special moment. Perhaps this is what Jesus meant when he said: "I tell you the truth, anyone who will not receive the Kingdom of God like a little child will never enter it" (Mark 10:15; Luke 18:17). What a peaceful sleep settles on our lives as we bed down in Grand Forks, North Dakota!

Journal, May 27th-June 2nd

With a longing backward look, we leave Grand Forks, the "Hi-Line," North Dakota, Montana, and the high plains. Though our spirits want to linger, we are reminded that journeys, physical or spiritual, must move forward. One of the most difficult lessons for us to learn is we must be willing to let go of whatever captures our hearts when Spirit calls us, like Abraham, to "go forth." Having been commissioned on this journey to *listen and follow,* we turn our eyes, as well as our hearts, eastward.

Wrapped in the familiar sylvan green of Minnesota after the exhilaration of riding the openness of the high plains, my emotions are beset with the clear awareness that this wonderful journey is entering its final phase. This clarity helps me understand why I begin to experience periods of depression as we ride through the woodlands of the northwestern part of the state and the Lost River State Park. The words of the psalmist rise like prayer in my heart: "My soul is weary with sorrow; strengthen me according to Your word" (Psalm 119:28). The sound of lake waters lapping at the shore sings a soothing song to my spirit as we enter Warroad, on the shores of Lake of the Woods. An inviting lakeside restaurant offers a lovely view while we enjoy a delicious meal before we search for nightly lodging.

I do not sleep well. I feel very tired when I awake this morning. Insomnia does not help my feelings of depression. Spiritually, it seems to be the time of descending from the "mountain top experience" in which I felt so fully loved by the Divine and sensed a tremendous upwelling of that Love in my own life. At the moment, however, the joy of that experience seems a distant dream. I feel ashamed to be encased in despair when we have been gifted with so much wonder and blessing. I must remember, however, that the spiritual journey does not always travel the gleaming transcendent mountaintops of experience, but the path often leads through the "valley of the shadow." My heart sighs a silent plea:

> As we ride through these miles and miles of trees,
> I feel lost in a forest; no way out do I see.
> Threatening to cover the brightness with increasing gloom,
> the clouds pile up and drift across the blue.
> Even the sun is blocked, shutting off the warmth,
> covering me with shadows.
> Spirit, please, with the oil of grace my head anoint.
> A wide peaceful river is sent
> to lend some calm to my troubled heart.

We pause for a snack at a rest stop along the rapidly flowing Rainy River. On the far bank lies the pastoral scene of Canadian farmlands. In the stillness, we sit and gaze at the river's strong, swift current that in some mysterious way seems to pick up my depression and carry it away.

As we ride on, I banish my thoughts and focus my attention on what is before me: the beauty of the Minnesota landscape along the water's edge. When we arrive at Rainy Lake, in International Falls, we find a rustic lodge overlooking the lake. The young woman who shows us our room is surprised to find we have been riding alone, just the two of us, for three months now. Her response to that is: "You must really like each other!" We do!

We settle into a quaint second floor room; the beauty and quiet is very restful. After a cup of coffee and a nap, we are drawn by the invitation of the lakeshore to come outside for a stroll. Twilight soon settles over the lake and the mosquitoes quickly send us scurrying for the shelter of our room. As the curtain of darkness descends, we crawl into our bed for a good night's rest.

On our first morning in the lodge, I look out of our small double windows upon a scene of breathless tranquility:

> Tiny flecks of stars float
> in a milky blue sky;
> streaks of whipped cream clouds uncover
> one bright lone star.
> A silver lake mirrors
> an upside down world.
> Silent breeze
> ruffles the water;
> rose tinted sky
> spills onto the lake,
> a duck floats by,
> leaves no wake
> ~ still ~
> it watches and waits.
> The rose glow of dawn
> spreads across the lake.
> All is breathless!
> That still moment
> in morning's symphony
> before the glory
> of dawn's rhapsody.

Morning begins to dawn. Night slips away and carries with it the remnants of my depression. Once again my heart sings:

A New Way to Ride–Listening and Following

A bright eastern star, the early morn's glow,
    the bird's waking dance, a duck's quiet ballet,
    magenta clouds herald the coming day.

Morning star fades and drifts away
    its peace work woven into our night;
    it leaves to the painted dawn on the lake
    to lay on our souls a moment of grace.

Spreading rays like gold dust on the rippling waves,
    a ball of fire rises over the trees.
    Radiance fills the world with morning light.

My soul cannot resist such beauty!
It lifts its song of praise to heaven.

Journal, June 3rd-4th

The Shapes of God 12

Looking through our windows here at Rainy Lake, Minnesota, we watch the sun birth the day. My morning devotional reading is from the Psalms and the book of Judges. I note how Biblical authors do not hesitate to voice their pain and feelings of despair. Their laments, however, consistently end in praise and thankfulness to the Divine Love and Goodness Who is ever faithful. Listening to their wisdom, I have gained the humble courage to write of my own moments of despair. Nevertheless, gloom does not carry the day and my spirit bursts forth in wonder and praise:

> God comes in the dawn's glory of the painted sky,
> > in red, purples, pinks, on the horizon lying,
> > in pale rose fringes of heavy gray clouds,
> > in glowing beams on lake's night shroud.
>
> God comes in the blaze of the morning sky,
> > in the heavy dark clouds floating so high,
> > in the stillness of the early pre-dawn,
> > in the gentle stare of a tiny fawn.
>
> God comes in the treetops now frosted in brilliance,
> > in their emerging from cover of night's silence,
> > in ripples on lake as wind breathes its song,
> > in birds dancing and floating as breeze carries them along.

Disappointingly, the radiant dawn does not issue in a sunlit day. Clouds ominously rush across the sky and throw shadows on our hope to explore this wilderness area. Shadows do not always last, however, and by late morning,

> God comes in sunlit glory and patches of blue,
>   in path of sparkling light over lake's gray hue,
>   in diamond dance of sparkles on the water's surface,
>   in birds echoing song, fulfilling Creator's purpose.

We pick up our riding gear and head out for the bike. Beset by a multitude of tiny insects as soon as we step outside, we are challenged to remember they too are a beloved part of the Creator's covenant:

> God comes in the dragonflies swirling around our heads,
>   in caterpillars eating tree leaves that on bike they shed,
>   in mosquitoes covering the screens on our windows,
>   in my pondering the purpose God has for each creature.

Clearing the bike of tree leaf litter, we brush aside the flying critters, pull on our helmets, and wave good-bye to our host. Stopping for lunch at a favorite local restaurant in Ranier, we whisper a prayer of thanks for the awareness of divine Presence in all of our activities.

> God comes in the warm sunshine of mid-day,
>   in smile of resort owner who invites us to stay,
>   in warmth of "Gramma's Pantry"
>   and smiles as we are served,
>   in the praise we give for Walleye dinner,
>   applause richly deserved.

Offering friendliness and delicious food, Gramma's Pantry is a wonderful find. Their specialty is Walleye, a local fish and a new taste treat for us. As we wait for our lunch, I walk over to a wall-sized bulletin board to look at the display. Am I ever surprised! The whole bulletin board is a photo and news article display of the life of their "native daughter," Tammy Faye Baker. The display is dedicated with "We love you Tammy Faye;" quite a tribute from this little Minnesota town.

Filled with warmth from the gracious people in "Gramma's Pantry," our hearts glow under the sunlit sky. We ride deep into the forest to visit the Voyageurs National Park Museum where we are introduced to the fascinating lifestyle of the "voyageurs" who trapped in this frozen wilderness many years ago. The museum is located in the Visitors Center, a gorgeous building of hewn logs, but virtually empty of tourists. Apparently winter is their tourist season during which they plow paths out to the frozen lake for the persons who enjoy ice fishing. Other favorite winter sports in the area are snowmobiling and cross-country skiing. Knowing the chilly average temperatures in this part of the nation, I admire the fortitude of these winter adventurers, but have little desire to participate.

Having greatly enjoyed our afternoon tour, we return to our quiet lodge. At the marina across the cove, we learn that summer recreation takes place far out on the lake. A favorite activity is floating along in a houseboat. Motorboats provide quicker access to the lake, but limit the amount of time one can spend far from shore. Leaving the cove in the early morning, these boats carve a slice into the still water; ripples disperse the floating glory of the morning sunrise mirrored on the lake. This area provides a wondrous variety of opportunity to enjoy the natural world. As our last full day here comes to a close, we savor the calm beauty and retreat to our cozy room to watch the gentle closing in of the night.

> God comes in the quiet of twilight's fall,
> > in the floating duck pair and their haunting calls,
> > in the slight bending of the graceful tall pines,
> > in the wind's lullaby at evening time.

Riding away from Rainy Lake this morning, I remain lost in a spirit of wonder and I become engaged in the game the sky is playing:

> Sky's gray mantle is being chased
> By the sun and the blue,
> Which are trying so hard now to break through.
> The white cotton clouds pick up the sun's rays.
> Which will decide the mood of the day?
>
> For a time, it seems the gray will win,
> But the sun persists;
> Earth glows from its kiss.
> The forest is bathed in shadow and light,
> Then once again the clouds roll in.
> As the clouds play tag, we ride in delight.

We are wrapped in the stillness and lush scents of Kabetogama State Forest and Superior National Forest. The serenity of our journey instills a tender appreciation for the scenes gracing our travel:

> Miles and miles of pine trees
> Rock walls ~ canvases of abstract art
> Muted colors of every sort
> Deer scurry to hide, white tails aloft
> This wilderness seems gentle and soft:
> Vision of tranquility flowing from Divine heart.

By late afternoon, our ride breaks free of the forest and we arrive in Ely, Minnesota. In the morning, we continue meandering through the woodlands while ducking in and out of towns named Isabella, Murphy City, and Finland. After some sixty miles, the road leaves the sheltering forest and astounds us with a view of Lake Superior. Following the Lake's jagged northern rim, we welcome the feel of the moist lake air and the open space. High above the Lake, we stop at an overlook walled around by boulders and fringed by bushes sprinkled with pink flowers and dancing green and rose leaves. Our spirits merge with the serenity of this place. A chipmunk, which seems to be longing for company of any species, scurries across the rocks, under our bike, and close enough for us to touch; but that he does not allow! We obviously do not have the necessary handout he would reward with such a privilege. Reluctantly, we leave this charming creature and this peaceful vista.

The tranquility of the lake road inspires reflection on how the beauty, scents, and sounds of nature have imprinted a sense of Spirit's presence upon our hearts. In this reflective mood, we enter the city of Duluth, Minnesota, located at the western tip of Lake Superior. Because our motel window provides only a restricted view of the lake, I am shut off from the outside and my spirit feels cramped. The time we spend walking the lakefront boardwalk is sheer joy. When the time comes to depart Duluth, I feel little reluctance in leaving, although it is a beautiful city. My spirit is aching to be in the world of nature once again.

Journal, June 6th-9th

Riding along the lake's southern shores, we are amazed at the size of this largest of the Great Lakes. Although the road soon exits Minnesota and enters Wisconsin, we still do not leave behind vast Lake Superior. Instead, we turn northeast to ride the rim of a large peninsula jutting far into the lake. Rounding the northern tip of the peninsula, we arrive in the lakeside town of Bayfield, Wisconsin. While we feast on a delicious fish sandwich, our eyes feast on the stunning view.

We would love to stay here, but since no place seems to present itself for overnight lodging, we climb onto the Wing and ride the circle of road heading out of town. Spirit has, however, held in abeyance a surprise we do not see until we round the last curve before exiting Bayfield. There, nestled on a bluff, is the small Sea Gull Bay Motel. The motel site provides an unfettered view of the lake and the Apostle Islands in the distance. When we inquire about a room, the owners tell us we are most fortunate because they have a cancellation for one night. Not only are we gifted with a room, but adding to our delight, the owners of this motel have designated it as a completely smoke-free property ~

A New Way to Ride–Listening and Following

no smoking allowed anywhere, even in the parking lot. This is a *first* in all of our travels.

We carry our bags into our little suite and walk onto our deck. Immersing ourselves in the glorious view, we realize there is a further gift: there are no lights on the side of the motel facing the lake. We know one night cannot possibly be enough; yet, one night is all the owners have free. We must be content and give thanks for what has been given. For the first time in two weeks, rather than peering through a window, we are able to sit outside and *feel* the natural world. We watch the changing face of the lake as twilight descends.

>The sky, once shining royal blue,
>now a pale whisper
>as twilight gathers.
>Bulbous white clouds float singularly ~
>then join into a party crowd.
>A heavy, gray bank rises
>from the lake's surface,
>to join cloud party.
>The sun, from its distant bedding den,
>laser paints the clouds,
>face-side with glowing pink,
>heads with rose curls
>that fade into pale purple and gray.
>The lake once sparkling, inviting,
>and filled with sails, ripples, and wake
>is now still.
>Its pewter surface,
>bare, free of human intrusion,
>reflects a muted twilight sky.
>Sprays of dusty rose clouds
>drop their beauty, flower girl like,
>in sprinkled paths across the lake.
>As sun departs, before night appears,
>lake, sky, earth,

lie in breezeless gray serenity.
One lone boat
makes wake on the molten surface,
rushesfrom the scene
embarrassed
to have broken the stillness.
It is the hush
in which Elijah heard the voice of God!
Do we too hear?

With this question lingering in our hearts, we open our spirits to hear and settle in for the night. We soon drift into a deep and restful sleep.

Having the opportunity to enjoy our pre-dawn coffee on our open deck under the cloud covered sky, I begin to understand some of the periods of depression I have been experiencing. We have had lovely places to stay where I could look out of my window to view the sky, the stars, the sunrises and sunsets. I was distanced, however, from the experience by window's glass barrier. Here on our deck, we watch the day being born and the sunrise glow touches us with a breath of warmth. It is for this my spirit has longed. Tasting the air, hearing the night and early morning sounds, listening to the rains, being baptized by the dews of the morning, and connecting with the radiance of the moon and stars, I am at one with all of creation and I bow in the Presence:

God is the moon ~
   hauntingly lustrous,
   reflecting Love's womb;
God is the star ~
   brilliantly glistening,
   beaming Light from afar
God is the sun ~
   blazingly bright,
   making my heart warm;
God is the rain ~

> refreshingly flowing,
> washing away pain;
> God is the fog ~
> enclosingly gray,
> embracing my song;
> God is that within ~
> seedingly present,
> making all of us kin.

We long to make this moment last! We do not want to leave this peaceful place! This one night, however, is the only vacancy they have. There is no sunrise to bid us adieu this morning; the clouds are much too thick. By the time it is light and we are ready for breakfast, it is raining ~ serious, heavy rain. Though we do not relish riding out in this rain, this time has been so wonderful we cannot find it in our hearts to complain, but only to be grateful.

> Amazing how God gifts our days,
> great love and care shown in so many ways.
> We sit with Mystery each early morn:
> Spirit comes, in breath of dawn.

And Spirit does come! With a gift! When we go to the office to check out, we ask, with little hope of an affirmative answer, if there have been any cancellations so that we might be able to stay another day. Why are we surprised to hear the answer? We will have to change rooms, but we may stay for another night. With joyful, thankful hearts, we pack and move. Soon the rain ends, the sun appears, and we are granted a glorious day. On this First Day morning, we settle into the silent worship of our Quaker tradition, our heads bowed in humble gratitude.

The day takes on a tranquil mood as we read, write postcards, walk in the sunshine, rest, and enjoy the beauty of the lake glistening in the sun. By late afternoon the lake takes on a different look. Heavy clouds settle over the Apostle Islands although elsewhere the sky is blue and the sun sparkles on the water. Soon the wind whips up, whitecaps appear, and boats speed toward shelter. Fog rolls in like a massive breath blown into icy air. The lake is soon obscured. A sailboat that failed to make harbor floats in the gray scene as though suspended in mid-air. Another wind gust sweeps the fog toward shore where it is pushed heavenward by the cliffs bordering our motel. A sudden appearance of the sun vaporizes the mist. Waves of fog roll in and out over the next several hours. Perched on the railing of our deck, the motel's resident robin seems bewildered at this strange atmospheric game.

At one point, when the fog has vanished, part of the sky becomes covered with heavy dark clouds. The sun pours brilliant rays beneath the clouds and bathes the lake and islands with lustrous glory. Then fog rolls in once again, and we watch as it moves slowly and gracefully toward us until it covers everything beyond the trees in front of our motel. A moist stillness falls; all is tranquil and quiet. The Divine Artist seems to have had a joyous time creating this Sabbath day masterpiece.

On our last morning in Bayfield, we sit on our deck to say our good-byes to this place of graced solitude. The fog is so dense there is no view beyond our railing:

> No red paints the sky this morn,
> no sound of waves upon shore born;
> no whispering of wind's soft voice:
> only stillness, quiet and moist.
>
> We fall on face and ask to hear,
> "What is the message this fog bears?"
> Mystery's answer: "Go ride in trust;
> way will be shown, but follow you must."

Having been given the command, we trustingly mount the Gold Wing and ride into

> Fog ~ the great Mystery!
> We peer and look, but cannot see;
> it is not given to human eyes
> to know what in the future lies.

Riding in fog is much like our spiritual journeys. Not only must we travel slowly and be intensely aware, but also

> embraced by the fog, we must content be,
> for the present is all that is given to see.
> The future is hidden in fog's mystery;
> the past fades into fog's gray drizzly sea.
>
> It is not frightening, but very still.
> We are held within the Eternal Will,
> wrapped in Mysterious cocoon,
> like beings held in Spirit's womb.

We emerge from this fog-laden cocoon as we leave the Wisconsin shoreline of Lake Superior. Bursting into the brilliant sun-bathed Upper Peninsula of Michigan, we travel inland scenes of forest, hills, rivers, and small lakes. This sylvan pathway leads us once again to the shores of Lake Superior and a night in Marquette, Michigan.

Journal 9th-11th

Leaving Marquette, the road through the Upper Peninsula forms a convoluted pathway rolling along the southern shores of Lake Superior, then dipping south through the sheltering Hiawatha National Forest, and finally opening onto the glistening shores of Lake Michigan. The golden beaches are strewn with large boulders washed clean by the gentle rolling surf. Over the sands fragile leafy vines blossom shiny yellow wildflowers. We are enthralled by this picturesque landscape.

We are to be treated, however, to delights other than the tranquil beaches. One delicious surprise is locally smoked salmon. Small, well-seasoned shacks appear periodically along the road advertising their one product ~ smoked salmon. Entering one of these establishments, we find an antique refrigerator case filled with what looks like toasted shoe leather. This first appearance causes us to cringe and we wonder if we will be jeopardizing our health to indulge. One bite of this smoked-on-the-site salmon resolves all questions. It is delicious! Our only regret is that we did not purchase more. We learn not to question the outward appearance in which blessings are dressed.

There is more! We stop in a small roadside restaurant for lunch and decide this is the time to feast on a local delicacy we have seen advertised for miles. A beef stew like mixture, wrapped in pastry and baked, these "Pasties" (I am laughingly informed that the proper pronunciation is "pass-tees") are delicious!

When we leave the restaurant after this hearty meal, we find the local sheriff waiting for us in his squad car. We are relieved to hear he has waited for our return to the Wing only to offer a friendly warning against riding over the Mackinaw Bridge this evening. Strong, dangerous winds are predicted for tonight. We thank him for this generous gift of his time and for the helpful warning. We also remember to be grateful for whatever guise Spirit uses to provide guidance.

Our day's journey culminates in St. Ignace, Michigan. There, shimmering in the sunlight stands the Mackinaw Bridge, a towering arch over the strait between Lake Michigan and Lake Huron that carries the traveler to the lower portion of Michigan. Locating a motel, we ask for a room with a view of the bridge. With delight, we walk into the penthouse with an open porch from which we have a spectacular view of both lakes as well as the bridge. The traffic creeping across the bridge in the howling wind is the scene that draws the curtain on our day. As a storm blows in, night descends.

After the rain, the pre-dawn sky is black. The bridge, magnificent with its luminous colored lights, drops sparkling

A New Way to Ride–Listening and Following

reflections over the dark waters. Sitting in wonder, we reflect on the message this scene speaks.

> The Mackinaw Bridge span rises high,
> beams red, green, and white lights into the sky.
> The morning is dark, clouds loom overhead,
> half moon breaks through to shed light on the bridge
> and the rising sun paints the clouds red.
>
> The bridge spans waters between two lakes,
> provides path from one life to another.
> Crossing this bridge is a treacherous journey ~
> mist and strong winds ~ we must travel slowly.
> With patient obedience to rules of the road,
> we are offered safe passage
> and new paths to explore.
>
> God builds the bridge and establishes the way,
> if we choose to cross the straits to new Life today.
> The progress is slow, the Way may strike fear,
> but steadily we move toward the Light on far shore.
> With Divine loving care,
> Our safe passage assured.

We must now depart to become participants in this vista we have enjoyed. Viewing from a distance is one thing. Becoming a part of that view is something else. Our blustery morning ride across the bridge is a breathtaking experience. The suspension towers of the bridge seem to rise hundreds of feet above us. The metal grates under the wheels of our Wing provide a view of the water far below. We feel as though we are looking down from a mountaintop. The wind whips the bike, and we both lean forward to lessen wind resistance. We are energized and exhilarated as we ride the descending slope on the far side of this magnificent bridge.

Our spirits, enlivened by this invigorating experience, soon wilt during a ride with long waits under a scorching sun on roads undergoing repair. Finally, released from our highway detention, we are gratified when the road winds its way along the eastern shore of Lake Michigan and then dips south to Grand Traverse Bay. At the southernmost point of the Bay, we decide to seek lodging for the night by riding up the lengthy peninsula in the center of the Bay. The road terminates at the Old Mission Lighthouse set in scenic beauty at the tip of the peninsula. A sign informs that we stand "on the 45th Parallel, halfway between the North Pole and the Equator." Hot and weary, we are singularly unimpressed by this unique privilege. Noting no overnight accommodations on our ride up the peninsula, we hoist our tired bodies onto our faithful Wing and begin the twenty-mile ride back to the mainland. We tell ourselves blessings sometimes come strangely disguised, but we really think in this case we were listening more to what we wanted than to our Guide.

Thoroughly fatigued, we arrive in Traverse City. Thankfully, Spirit remains true and we are led to a comfortable, air-conditioned suite located right on the beach. The simple pleasures of walking in gentle surf, resting, reading, and being present to the ever-changing face of the created world provide refreshment and unparalleled beauty:

>On the placid bay
>In predawn light
>Water and sky blend
>Leave no horizon
>No line
>Between universe
>And planet earth.
>
>Ducks float by
>Leave slight wake.
>Rose glow of dawn
>Unfurls night's curtain
>And shore lights dim
>As sun's rise births the day.
>Orange fireball

Breaks the horizonless scene
Pours glimmers upon the lake
Releases sparkles from sands of shore.

Lost in the glory of this sunrise moment,
We feel held in the wonder of Creation's community.

    Though the days continue to be hot and muggy with only a slight breeze brushing the air, the heat never despoils our joy during our time in Traverse City. On our last morning, we sit on the beach in the motionless warm air. The moon and morning star are the only bright fixtures in the sky. The other stars give forth only a slight, fuzzy glow through the haze. The dawn paints a pale, pink streak across the gray/rose sky. The glowing orange sun enters the scene as though emerging from the mist. As the sun rises higher in the sky, a royal, fluorescent, scarlet/orange runner spreads across the lake to the shore like a royal carpet into the heavens. An image to carry with us into this day's journey!

Journal, June 11th-15th

THE JOURNEY CONTINUES

The time in Traverse City "restores our souls" (Psalm 23:3). Today's ride continues that pattern. We weave through woodlands cut through by rivers and dotted with small lakes around which have clustered tiny cottages and lodges. On the shore of one of these lakes, we stop to have a snack while we absorb the scenic beauty. We watch as a couple glide away in their canoe. As their bark breaks the pristine surface, they leave behind a rippling wake that spreads across the water.

The humid heat of summer lies like a moist blanket; this type of weather condition is conducive to the strong thunderstorms predicted for the afternoon. As morning begins to press upon the noon hour, thick black clouds congregate in the sky. Yet, this menacing sky teases us with glimpses of sunshine. Inevitably, however, the clouds thicken and we know that we must quickly find shelter.

Once again, we are graced with the "perfect" place. Searching as we ride, our eyes catch sight of a group of log cabins, early 1950's vintage, tucked back from the road near the woods ~ quaint, rustic, homey. After making arrangements for our night's lodging, we ride to a nearby farmer's market/restaurant to feast on fresh Broasted (local fare) Alaskan Pollock. Fresh homemade "mountain" bread is the treasure we carry back to our cabin. Dodging the hoard of mosquitoes as best we can, we unpack, put the bike to bed, and set a pot of coffee on to brew.

A New Way to Ride–Listening and Following

> Tucked away in our tiny log cabin,
> dry and warm, we have what we need.
> In dewy quietness, the soft rains come
> filling the air with moisture, refreshing the day.
> Music of dripping rain-sounds soothes our spirits.

The sound of rain on the cabin roof lulls us into a restful slumber. Waking in the stillness of late afternoon, we savor the sweetness of our surroundings:

> A portrait of beauty is framed in each cabin window:
> tall graceful pines, drooping hemlocks, lacy maples,
> red and white petunias, lavender roses.
> By all of these scenes, our spirits are blessed.

Snug in our cozy little hermitage, we watch the night wrap its sheltering coverlet over the day and listen to the

> symphony of raindrops serenading our evening;
> dull plush on the roof, syncopated blips from the eves,
> splish in the puddles, and splush as drops hit leaves.

> For us tonight, the rain is Joy,
> Just one part of God's world, all of which is holy.

The rain forms a moist cocoon around our little cabin and lullabies us into a deep and refreshing sleep.

In the morning, after the rain has ended, the scene from our windows lifts our spirits to joyful praise:

> Dark green trees
> against crisp blue sky,
> white, soft clouds,
> sun so high,
> the air
> fresh, clear, and pure:
> Spirit bathed the world with showers
> our haze to cure.

Journal, June 15th

Riding away from our cabin near Manistee, Michigan, we watch the clouds move across the sky only to be chased away by the sun. The brightness lasts but a short time before clouds move in again. We are as unsure of the weather as we are of the events into which we ride this day.

> We know not
> what the day will bring,
> but gray clouds cannot dampen
> the joy our hearts sing.

We travel the road south toward Big Rapids, Michigan, where we will visit with Fred's relatives. After months of treasured solitude, we wonder how it will feel to be suddenly enveloped in the busyness, togetherness, and joyousness of family life. We are greeted with an overwhelmingly warm welcome! Though our plan is to stay only one day and night, the family insists we stay at least through Father's Day weekend. We cannot resist this embracing love.

Our relatives live in a bustling urban community, but their home is cloistered in the rural-like setting of a quiet suburban area. Their wooden deck looks over a pond on which float the pads and blooms of water lilies. While the numinous quality of this place offers a setting for silence and meditation, we are hard pressed to be able to snatch even a few such moments. The joy of our relatives in having us visit overflows and we are drawn in, with reciprocal joy, to constant conversations, a happy family gathering, and delicious feasting.

On Father's Day morning, we wake to a magnificent scene that carries Divine Spirit's message of love for creation:

> In the morning ~ dark and still,
> smell of rain, nostrils fill;
> blast of lightning bathes the sky,
> thunder crashes, sounds vibrate high;
> bouncing of raindrops on wooden deck,
> morning dance

of moistness' effect;
the lake, a mass of sprinkled puddles.

Sun begins to wake the day,
sky turns blue, gray clouds drift away.
Blowing in, white cloud puffs glow
with hidden sunrise pink and rose.
Slowly now, the rain subsides;
each single raindrop bounces
ripples upon the pond
that spread and hide
among the lily pads.
Are these Holy tears
wept for a world so sad?

Contemplating this message, we sit in silent prayer. All is so quiet we can almost hear the raindrops fall into the pond.

From this momentary solitude, we move into celebrating the day with family. Later in the morning the storm moves on and the sun appears. Fred readies to take Cousin Madeline for a motorcycle ride, something she very much wants to do. Suddenly, however, she gets "cold feet" and tries to wiggle out of going. Encouraged by her husband, Cousin Albert, she takes this opportunity to fulfill her dream. Suited up and all smiles, she rides off with Fred on our Gold Wing. She returns ecstatic! The rest of the day we spend in festivity with the extended family, most of whom we have never met. As we share experiences and stories, we feel deeply graced.

A glorious Father's Day we spend!
The day is sunny, cool, and clear;
breeze floats gently through the air.
We talk and talk and talk all day,
Laugh and eat; that is our play.

We carry the warm glow of this time in our hearts as we retire for the night, but we admit we are fatigued and looking forward to returning to the aloneness of our journey.

With hugs and thanks, we bid good-bye to family on the morning after Father's Day.

> "Salt of the earth,"
> fine folk they are,
> people of faith, patriotic to a flaw.
> This is Fred's family! Joyous two days!
> Can we be so happy to be on our way?
>
> *Journal, June 16th-17th*

Almost as though having experienced a page out of time, we return to our contemplative journey. This day is truly a challenge to our commitment to accept whatever path we are given as *gift*.

> Across the state we head east,
> away from conversation and feast.
> Dark clouds accompany us all day
> along the repaired, being improved, road way.
> Spirits struggle as we inch along
> to turn this ride into Creator's song.

On the torturously slow ride and interminable waits for road work to proceed, we try to elicit a sense of peace from whatever scenes of loveliness are provided.

> Winds blow strong across open space,
> Divine call our hearts and minds to claim.
> Gentle farms, lakes, and trees appear,
> our spirits calm and the ride yields peace.
> Solitude is given us once again in creation.
> In listening and looking, we see *all* as wonder.

The months of contemplative riding and awareness of God's presence in everything do not seem to make it less difficult to accept the ordinariness of today's ride straight across Michigan to Port Huron. Our trip seems more like riding-to-get-somewhere than riding to immerse ourselves in the rhythmic song of nature. Yet, even here is a lesson for us: most of life is composed of the "ordinariness" of days and Spirit invests those days with holiness also. The reality of divine Presence embodying all moments of life is experientially impressed upon my spirit. I must simply be open to that Presence.

We welcome the much needed night's rest in Port Huron. This morning greets us with another day of "ordinariness" on interstate highway leading through Ontario.

> Riding the strip, we cross Canada,
> wind whipping our helmets,
> pushing the bike and us.
> Beautiful farmland,
> planted fields sprouting green,
> mile upon mile
> of this peaceful scene.
>
> Peace on the road is not to be found.
> Trucks barrel by,
> vacuums twist us around;
> road work bedevils,
> roads are a hazard;
> traffic constantly roars:
> no leisure; no pleasure.

I try to remember and live into my reflections of last evening. A prayer lifts from my heart: "This is the path we are given; help me rejoice in it!"

> Peace is found only within our souls:
> center down;
> joy in the wind-twists,
> noise, and bouncy road!
> These externals are our reality,
> but within
> Spirit nurtures the calm of Eternity.

We stop only once on this lengthy highway, about half way across, to refuel the Wing with gas and us with coffee and doughnuts. Somewhat refreshed, we return to the ride.

> The scenery doesn't vary:
> tranquil farms and trees.
> This landscape plays on
> with monotonous ease.

Daydreaming takes over; the poetry begins to flow and I start scribbling notes. Completely absorbed in my writing, I lose touch with the scenes all around me until

> suddenly ~
> a wind gust lifts helmet
> nearly off my head, and I know
> Spirit is saying,
> "Stop writing and look where you are led!"
> Pen and pad go in pocket,
> helmet shield is locked down.
> Spirit's voice in the wind
> shuts out all other sound.

Though my focus is set on the distant vision of Niagara Falls, Spirit awakens me to messages of beauty in the scenes surrounding us as we travel. I *listen*! As I become more attentive to the moment, I find the trip becomes more pleasant and the scenes elicit more joy in my spirit.

Journal, June 18th-19th

Early in the afternoon, we arrive safely in Niagara Falls, New York, and settle comfortably into a room overlooking the magnificent Niagara River. Later, as we walk by the river and watch its power as it flows to the falls, I recall the words of an Irishman who, as he walked by the sea, said it made him feel "very wee," but he was happy. We feel more than happiness; a deep joy fills us as we stand awed before the majesty of this river. We are humbled by the message it speaks to our lives:

> A mighty river flows through the land
> to speak the Word from Creator's hand.
> The mighty Niagara rushes toward the falls;
> in its voice, I hear God's call.
>
> As I stand before this mighty force,
> its power alone serves to quiet my voice.
> Its roar fills my soul with awe!
> The only response ~ on my knees to fall.
>
> No question that in the grip of its power,
> there is total loss of control; the thought makes me cower.
> I like to be master of my own fate,
> A pipe dream ~ I'm learning of late.
>
> It is joy that I feel as I watch this river rush
> unimpeded to the falls, over the cliff without blush,
> to be shattered and broken and burst into foam,
> sending mist high to the sky, its heavenly home.
>
> A mighty river of Divine love sweeps into my heart,
> carries away emotional debris and clutter of all sorts.
> This experience of Infinite love filling my life
> washes over the falls all manner of strife.
>
> To allow this Great River of love to flow into my life,
> I must relinquish control to Spirit's guiding Light,
> be swept toward the falls, where self-will is shattered,
> be absorbed in the mist of the Eternal Agenda.

Our hearts radiant with Spirit's presence emanating from this mighty river, we walk quietly back to our motel. We had planned this layover simply because we wanted to visit the American side of the Falls. We discover, however, that our spiritual journey has not come to an end, but instead is moving toward an exhilarating contemplative climax.

We are being drawn into a deep meditative communion with the Life infusing this magical landscape. Standing at our window as evening comes, we are awed at the unfolding scene:

The Journey Continues

Human lights
illumine the entire vista;
to chase away nature's darkness,
they are insistent:
colored lights mist over the Falls,
brilliant beams irradiate bridges,
choreographed illusions dance on buildings,
and luminaries bathe all of night's edges.

Lightning
suddenly fills the sky with a glow,
as a storm
begins to grow.
We watch from our window
as the clouds gather, and
the majestic sunset colors
begin to scatter.

The storm,
comes closer, echoes thunder,
streaks lightning across the sky.
Before this brandishing of nature's energy,
town lights fade into shadows;
human light remains
a feeble glow.

An example
of Who is in control!
One streak of lightning breaks
skyline lights' hold, plunges city
into the darkness it fears,
and wipes out
its lighted cheer.

As the majesty
of lightning rips across the sky,
our eyes sparkle with wonder
at the power it supplies.
In the beauty

of all of nature's strange ways
God's love is present.
Let us give praise!

We go to bed wrapped in wonder, as we marvel at creation.

Our one full day in Niagara Falls is electric with the vitality of a landscape bidding us come and participate fully. We do! Our first visit is to Cave Of The Winds where, donned in slippers and rain slicks, we enter the waters:

We walk the wooden path
at the foot of the falls.
Spirit's voice thunders:
"Come stand and be blessed
by this water;
know yourselves the beloved children
of our Heavenly Father."

Our feet are washed
by the flow of the falls
as it pours over the walkway,
splashing us all,
crashing on rocks,
bursting forth with a thrust;
we linger as the waterflood sprays
its beauty upon us.

We stand face up in the wind and roar and mist to be literally baptized by this mighty river plummeting over the Bridal Veil Falls:

Beneath the falls
on the Hurricane Deck,
soaked to the skin
we stand,
before this Power
only tiny specks.
We rejoice in this baptism
of majestic Love,

> feel free, renewed, thankful
> for this Grace from above.

Emerging from this experience drenched, we walk into the glorious sunshine and feel new life bursting within us.

After a change of clothes and a delicious lunch, we walk to stand in silent wonder before the power and unparalleled grandeur of Horseshoe Falls. As the day begins to wane, we are drawn again to the scene that has most profoundly touched our spirits: the inexpressibly chaotic beauty of the Niagara River, alive with the immanent Presence of the Eternal.

> As we watch the river, it dawns upon us,
> "All glorious chaos is but majesty!"
> Waves tumble, roll, smash
> into one another,
> jump over rocks, splash into air,
> and roll backwards on each other.

> As we ponder this scene with joy and wonder,
> we realize this chaos
> is really God's order:
> exciting and exhilarating,
> refreshingly new, never the same,
> always becoming,
> to itself ever true.
> Humankind likes things neat,
> orderly, controlled, in bounds:
> if this were our river,
> it would be boringly sound.
> All smooth with manicured edges,
> waves moving the same, unruffled water flow
> feeling and causing no pain.

> We celebrate the joy
> of a surprising conclusion:
> Divine order is different,
> a seeming mass of confusion;

in this tumbling array of differing waves,
the Creator breaks into human lives
with Truth that saves.

To bring our contemplative journey to an illuminating climax, the Master Creator seems to pour the music of divine Presence into the thundering, splashing, renewing beauty of the Niagara River and Falls. With the soul-lifting experience of this day still alive within, we look once more at the glistening lights on the Falls and then close our eyes to sleep in peace.

Journal, June 19th-20th

From this high moment, we ease our hearts into the final portion of our trip. We ride south to spend a few days with dear friends in Erie, Pennsylvania. During the visit, we joy in simple pleasures: sharing meals, having afternoon coffee and conversation on their deck, and going out in the evenings for a cone of our favorite ice cream ~ Rocky Mountain Raspberry. Together we tour Erie to see the colorful fish sculptures adorning the city and locate the brick commemorating our friends' contribution to downtown development. On the last day of our visit, we take a chilly, stormy cruise on Lake Erie. Before retiring that evening, I reflect on the pleasure of these days and the deep richness and value of

Friendship ~
treasured over many years,
forged through sharing of laughter and tears.
We are given friends who enrich our lives
and help us understand
love-sharing for which life strives.

Jesus called the disciples
His friends
and shared with them the riches God lends.
He left a command
to love one another as He loved,

a challenge
which can be met only
through Grace from above.

We must respect one another,
love each as one's self,
see that of God
in each person and build communities of trust.
All become friends
as we share
Divine goodness and love.
As communities of friends spread,
the whole world is blessed.

Having shared the warm hospitality of our friends for several days, we wave good-bye as our Wing rolls down their driveway into the street. Soon we are on the main highway heading toward the Southeast through the familiar green hills of Pennsylvania and finally to Cumberland, Maryland. There we stay overnight in a little motel, beside a bubbling brook and under the shadow of a mountain.

Journal, June 21st-24th

We wake to the sound of the brook bouncing over the rocks as it rushes along its path. When we look out of the window,

morning has broken
brilliant and clear:
sun shining,
sky blue,
air fresh from rain's cheer.
Fog hangs on the mountain
and glistens in the sun
like the mystery of our lives when
to God's love we are won.

We dress slowly and pack the bike. Riding to a restaurant just across the highway, we enjoy pancakes, eggs and sausage courtesy of our motel. It is time now to begin the final leg of this journey. We pull on our helmets for the last time and climb onto our Gold Wing.

> Road to home stretches out before us,
> The draw is one of longing
> And a feeling so joyous.

We soon leave the foggy cool of the Maryland mountains and descend into the warmer flatlands of Virginia. Aware that this is our last day on the road, we reflect upon the experience of living into this "new way to ride" ~ *listening and following* ~ and the significance it has for our lives:

> Four months now we've been away
> being blessed by Creator each and every day.
> The beauty we've seen
> has entered our souls
> and provided spiritual blessings,
> values untold.

In divine Presence abiding, we have ridden each day;
we have trusted Spirit's guidance to lead the way.

We truly have been given a "new way to ride," but it will not be folded away into the trunk of our Gold Wing until our next tour because it has taken hold of us as a way of living.

> Our prayer, as we continue this trek to our home,
> is that lessons learned,
> we will keep trusting
> in Spirit's guidance alone.
> Each morning may we continue to offer our day
> to God's hands
> and then do
> what divine Will has planned.
>
> For that is our only and everyday task:
> Humbly following along the divinely inspired Path.

The Journey Continues

In the quiet late morning, exactly four months from the day we departed, we pull into the driveway of our retreat-like home to be greeted by the deer, the blackberries, and later, the star-sprinkled carpet of night above our deck. As we settle into the comfort of our home environment, we prayerfully give thanks for being *led* into this journey of wonder, for our safe return home, and for the gift that issued from my call to be a *traveling contemplative* ~

Poetry ~
which has flowed the entire time on the road
as creation has spoken God's Word to our souls.

What we have learned for our own spiritual life
has come as a deeply abiding insight:
Spirit provides the messengers to speak the Word;
humans or books or creation ~ none must be spurned.

I've tried to be faithful to write what I was given
as creation's wonder exposed our hearts to heaven.
Whether the message has been for one alone
or for a greater use
is God's choice.

These words I have written are now offered to all,
a gift of my responding faithfully
to God's *call* to a path
that for me was a very new way.
May Spirit use my offering
To touch some heart today.

Journal, June 25th

We thank all of you who have given us the privilege of sharing this "new way to ride/live" with you. We pray God's blessing on all of us as we journey ~ *listening and following.*

NOTES

* Brother Lawrence, *The Practice of the Presence of God.* (Grand Rapids, MI: Fleming H. Revell Co., 1958).

** Wendy Wright, *The Time Between.* (Nashville, TN: Upper Room Books, 1999), 114.

Appendix A:
Trip Itinerary & Routes

2/25 – From home - I-95s sixty miles to Exit 104 north of Richmond, VA

2/26 – From Richmond, VA - I-95s to overnight in Fayetteville, NC

2/27-28 – From Fayetteville, NC - I-95s then I-20w – Two nights in Columbia, SC

3/01-03 – From Columbia, SC – I-20w then Rt.441 – Three nights in Madison, GA with family

3/04 – From Madison, GA – Rt.441/129s then I-75s to overnight in Valdosta, GA

3/05-09 – From Valdosta, GA – I-75s then Rt.129 – Five nights in McAlpin, FL with family

3/10 – From McAlpin, FL – Rt.129 then Rt.27 then Rt.98 to overnight in Apalachicola, FL

3/11-12 – From Apalachicola, FL – Rt.98 – Two nights in Pensacola Beach, FL

3/13 – From Pensacola Beach, FL – Rt.98 then Rt.292 then Rt.161 then Rt.180 then Rt.90 to overnight in Pascagoula, MS

3/14 – From Pascagoula, MS – Rt.90 then I-10w then I-12w then I-10w to overnight in Baton Rouge, LA

3/15 – From Baton Rouge, LA – I-10w to overnight in Beaumont, TX

3/16-18 – From Beaumont, TX – I-10w – Three nights in Houston, TX visiting family and friends

3/19 – From Houston, TX – I-10w to overnight in San Antonio, TX visiting friends

3/20 – From San Antonio, TX – Rt.90 to overnight in Del Rio, TX

3/21 – From Del Rio, TX – Rt.90 to overnight in Marathon, TX

3/22-23 – From Marathon, TX – Rt.90 then I-10w then Rt.20 then I-10 – Two nights in El Paso, TX

3/24-25 – From El Paso, TX – I-10 then Rt.178 then Rt.9 then Rt.80 then Rt.90 – Two nights in Sierra Vista, AZ

3/26-29 – From Sierra Vista, AZ – Rt.90 then Tombstone Charleston Rd. then Rt.80 – Four nights in Holy Trinity Monastery, St. David, AZ

3/30-31 – From St. David, AZ – Rt.80 then I-10 – Two nights in Phoenix, AZ

4/01 – From Phoenix, AZ – I-10 to overnight in Blythe, CA

4/02 – From Blythe, CA – I-10 to overnight in Palm Springs, CA

4/03-05 – From Palm Springs, CA – Rt.111s then Rt.74 then I-5 – Three nights in San Diego, CA

4/06-07 – From San Diego, CA – I-8e – Two nights in El Centro, CA; day ride to Yuma, AZ

4/08 – From El Centro, CA – Rt.111n then Rt.78 then I-10e to overnight in Blythe, CA

4/09 – From Blythe, CA – Rt.95n to overnight in Needles, CA

4/10- From Needles, CA – I-40w then 95n to overnight in Las Vegas, NV

4/11-13 – From Las Vegas, NV – Rt.95n then Rt.373s then Rt.190w – Three nights in Furnace Creek, Death Valley, CA

4/14 – From Furnace Creek – Rt.190w to overnight in Panamint Springs, Death Valley, CA

Appendix A: Trip Itinerary & Routes

4/15 – From Death Valley, CA – Rt.190w then 395s then 178w to overnight in Bakersfield, CA

4/16 – From Bakersfield, CA – Rt.99s then I-5 then west through Frazier Park, then south to Rt.33 then Rt.101nw to overnight in Santa Barbara, CA

4/17 – From Santa Barbara, CA – Rt.101n then Rt.1n to overnight in Pismo Beach, CA

4/18 – From Pismo Beach, CA – Rt.101n then Rt.1n then Rt.46e then Rt.101n to overnight in Salinas, CA

4/19-20 – From Salinas, CA – Rt.101n – Two nights in San Mateo, CA

4/21-25 – Trip home – Five nights in Lake Ridge, VA

4/26 – From San Mateo, CA – Rt.92w then Rt.1n then Rt.101n then Rt.1n then east from Tomales to overnight in Petaluma, CA

4/27-28 – From Petaluma, CA – Rt.101n to Santa Rosa then Rt.101s to I-80e – Two days in the California mountains with friends

4/29 – From the mountains – Rt.20w then Rt.101s to overnight in Ukiah, CA

4/30 – From Ukiah, CA – West through the Montgomery Woods State Reserve to overnight in Mendocino, CA at the Sea Gull Inn

5/01 – From Mendocino, CA – Rt.1n then Rt.101n to overnight in Garberville, CA

5/02-04 – From Garberville, CA – West through Redway & Briceland – Three nights in Shelter Cove, CA

5/05 – From Shelter Cove, CA – East to Rt.101n to overnight in Eureka, CA

5/06-07 – From Eureka, CA – Rt.101n – Two nights in Crescent City, CA

5/08 – From Crescent City, CA – Rt.101n to overnight in Coos Bay, OR

A New Way to Ride–Listening and Following

5/09 – From Coos Bay, OR – Rt.101n to overnight in Florence, OR

5/10-11 – From Florence, OR – Rt.101n – Two nights in Newport, OR

5/12 – From Newport, OR – Rt.101n to Fort Clatsop National Monument and overnight

in Astoria, OR

5/13-14 – From Astoria, OR – Rt.101n – Two nights in Aberdeen, WA

5/15-16 – From Aberdeen, WA – Rt.109w to the coast then backtrack to Rt.101n – Two nights in Kalaloch, WA at Kalaloch Lodge

5/17-19 – From Kalaloch, WA - Rt.101n&e – Three nights in Port Angeles, WA at the

Uptown Motel. Side trip on Rt.112w to Neah Bay, WA and Cape Flattery

5/20 – From Port Angeles, WA – Rt.101e then Rt.20n then Ferry ride then Rt.20n to overnight in Mt. Vernon, WA

5/21 – From Mt. Vernon, WA – Rt.20e through Cascades National Park to overnight in Mazama, WA at the Freestone Inn

5/22-23 – From Mazama, WA – Rt.20e then Rt.155e then Rt.174e then Rt.2e – Two nights in Spokane, WA

5/24 – From Spokane, WA – Rt.2e to overnight in Libby, MT

5/25-26 – From Libby, MT – Rt.2e – Two nights in West Glacier, MT at Glacier National Park

5/27 – From West Glacier, MT – Rt.2e (The "High Line") to overnight in Havre, MT

5/28 – From Havre, MT – Rt.2e to overnight in Glasgow, MT

5/29 – From Glasgow, MT – Rt.2e to overnight in Williston, ND

Appendix A: Trip Itinerary & Routes

5/30-6/01 – From Williston, ND – Rt.2e – Three nights in Minot, ND

6/02 – From Minot, ND – Rt.2e to overnight in Grand Forks, ND

6/03 – From Grand Forks, ND – I-29n then Rt.11e to overnight in Warroad, MN

6/04-05 – From Warroad, MN – Rt.11e then Rt.71/11 – Two nights in International Falls, MN at Rainy Lake

6/06 – From International Falls, MN – Rt.53s then Rt.1e then Rt.1/169e to overnight in Ely, MN

6/07-08 – From Ely, MN – Rt.1s then Rt.61sw – Two nights in Duluth, MN

6/09-10 – From Duluth, MN – Rt.53s then Rt.13e – Two nights in Bayfield, WI in the Sea Gull Bay Motel

6/11 – From Bayfield, WI – Rt.13s then Rt.2e then Rt.28e then Rt.41e to overnight in Marquette, MI

6/12 – From Marquette, MI – Rt.41e then Rt.28e then Rt.77s then Rt.2e to overnight in St. Ignace, MI overlooking the Straits of Mackinac

6/13-14 – From St. Ignace, MI – I-75s then Rt.31s then round trip on Rt.37n to Old Mission and return to overnight in Traverse City, MI

6/15 – From Traverse City, MI – Rt.22n then Rt.204w then Rt.22s then Rt.109 then Rt.22s then Rt.31s to overnight south of Manistee, MI in a log cabin

6/16-17 – From Manistee, MI – Rt.31s the Rt.10e then Rt.131s – Two nights in Big Rapids, MI with family

6/18 – From Big Rapids, MI – Rt.131s then Rt.46e then I-75s then I-69e to overnight in Port Huron, MI

6/19-20 – From Port Huron, MI – Canadian Rt.402e then Rt.401e then Rt.403e then

QEW then Rt.405e into the United States – Two nights in Niagara Falls, NY

6/21-23 – From Niagara Falls, NY – I-190s then I-90w then I-79n – Three nights in Erie, PA visiting friends

6/24 – From Erie, PA – I-79s then I-68e to overnight in Cumberland, MD

6/25 – From Cumberland, MD – I-68e then I-70e then Rt.15s then I-66e then Rt.234s then Prince William Parkway east to HOME!

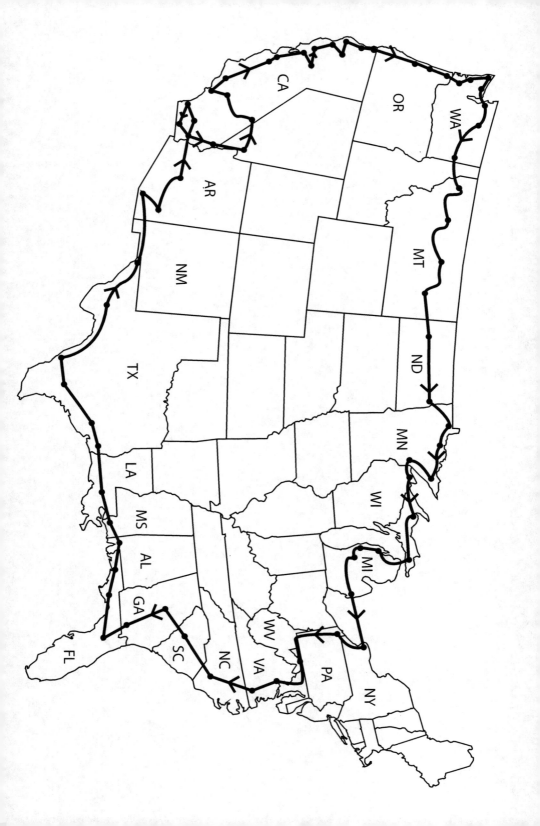

To order copies of

A New Way to Ride:
Listening & Following

see

http://www.geocities.com/judyceppa

or

contact Christy

at

judyceppa@gmail.com

or

304-725-3212

$12 +Shipping & Handling